**TEACHER'S PET PUBLICATIONS**

LITPLAN TEACHER PACK
for
The Pigman
based on the book by
Paul Zindel

Written by
Mary B. Collins

© 1996 Teacher's Pet Publications
All Rights Reserved

This **LitPlan** for Paul Zindel's
The Pigman
has been brought to you by Teacher's Pet Publications, Inc.

Copyright Teacher's Pet Publications 1996
11504 Hammock Point
Berlin MD 21811

Only the student materials in this unit plan
such as worksheets, study questions, assignment sheets, and tests
may be reproduced multiple times for use in the purchaser's classroom.

For any additional copyright questions,
contact Teacher's Pet Publications.

www.tpet.com

TABLE OF CONTENTS - The Pigman

Introduction	5
Unit Objectives	8
Reading Assignment Sheet	9
Unit Outline	10
Study Questions (Short Answer)	13
Quiz/Study Questions (Multiple Choice)	20
Pre-reading Vocabulary Worksheets	33
Lesson One (Introductory Lesson)	47
Nonfiction Assignment Sheet	49
Oral Reading Evaluation Form	52
Writing Assignment 1	56
Writing Assignment 2	66
Writing Assignment 3	70
Writing Evaluation Form	67
Vocabulary Review Activities	58
Extra Writing Assignments/Discussion ?s	59
Unit Review Activities	71
Unit Tests	75
Unit Resource Materials	107
Vocabulary Resource Materials	121

A FEW NOTES ABOUT THE AUTHOR
PAUL ZINDEL

ZINDEL, PAUL Paul Zindel was born in 1938 in Staten Island, New York. When he was two, his father left his family to live with a woman he had met on his police beat. As a practical nurse and with a few side jobs, Mr. Zindel's mother, Beatrice, made enough money to raise him and his older sister.

Paul Zindel contracted tuberculosis during his junior year at Port Richmond High School. He was sent to a sanitorium for treatment and could not return to school for eighteen months. He did complete his high school education and went on to receive a B. S. in chemistry and an M. S. in education from Wagner College.

Mr. Zindel's working career began at Allied Chemical Company, where he was a technical writer. Later, he taught chemistry and physics at Tottenville High School on Staten Island. After the success of his play The Effect of Gamma Rays on Man-in-the-Moon Marigolds, he left teaching to devote all of his time to writing.

Some of Mr. Zindel's most noteworthy works are *The Effect of Gamma Rays on Man-in-the-Moon Marigolds* (first produced in 1965, won Pulitzer Prize in 1971), *The Pigman* (1968), *My Darling, My Hamburger* (1969), *I Never Loved Your Mind* (1970), *Pardon Me, You're Stepping on My Eyeball* (1976), *Confessions of a Teenage Baboon* (1977), *The Undertaker's Gone Bananas* (1978), *The Pigman's Legacy* (1980), *Harry and Hortense at Hormone High* (1984), and *The Amazing and Death-Defying Diary of Eugene Dingman* (1987).

INTRODUCTION

This unit has been designed to develop students' reading, writing, thinking, and language skills through exercises and activities related to *The Pigman* by Paul Zindel. It includes seventeen lessons, supported by extra resource materials.

The **introductory lesson** introduces students to one main theme of the novel through a bulletin board activity. Following the introductory activity, students are given a transition to explain how the activity relates to the book they are about to read. Following the transition, students are given the materials they will be using during the unit. At the end of the lesson, students begin the pre-reading work for the first reading assignment.

The **reading assignments** are approximately thirty pages each; some are a little shorter while others are a little longer. Students have approximately 15 minutes of pre-reading work to do prior to each reading assignment. This pre-reading work involves reviewing the study questions for the assignment and doing some vocabulary work for 8 to 10 vocabulary words they will encounter in their reading.

The **study guide questions** are fact-based questions; students can find the answers to these questions right in the text. These questions come in two formats: short answer required or multiple choice-matching-true/false. The short answer version of the study questions comes in two styles: a short style which leaves no room for student responses (Students write answers on their own paper to conserve school supplies.) or a long style which does leave room for student responses. The best use of these materials is probably to use the short answer version of the questions as study guides for students (since answers will be more complete), and to use the multiple choice-matching-true/false version for occasional quizzes. If your school has the appropriate machinery, it might be a good idea to make transparencies of your answer keys for the overhead projector.

The **vocabulary work** is intended to enrich students' vocabularies as well as to aid in the students' understanding of the book. Prior to each reading assignment, students will complete a two-part worksheet for approximately 8 to 10 vocabulary words in the upcoming reading assignment. Part I focuses on students' use of general knowledge and contextual clues by giving the sentence in which the word appears in the text. Students are then to write down what they think the words mean based on the words' usage. Part II nails down the definitions of the words by giving students dictionary definitions of the words and having students match the words to the correct definitions based on the words' contextual usage. Students should then have a thorough understanding of the words when they meet them in the text.

After each reading assignment, students will go back and formulate answers for the study guide questions. Discussion of these questions serves as a review of the most important events and ideas presented in the reading assignments.

After students complete reading the work, there is a **vocabulary review** lesson which pulls together all of the fragmented vocabulary lists for the reading assignments and gives students a review of all of the words they have studied.

Following the vocabulary review, a lesson is devoted to the **extra discussion questions/writing assignments**. These questions focus on interpretation, critical analysis and personal response, employing a variety of thinking skills and adding to the students' understanding of the novel.

The **group activity** which follows the discussion questions has students working in small groups to discuss the main themes of the novel. Using the information they have acquired so far through individual work and class discussions, students get together to further examine the text and to brainstorm ideas relating to the themes of the novel.

The group activity is followed by a **reports and discussion** session in which the groups share their ideas about the themes with the entire class; thus, the entire class is exposed to information about all of the themes and the entire class can discuss each theme based on the nucleus of information brought forth by each of the groups.

There are **three writing assignments** in this unit, each with the purpose of informing, persuading, or having students express personal opinions. The first assignment is to inform: students explain to a classmate how to do a hobby. The second assignment is to persuade: students attempt to persuade a friend/acquaintance not to carry out a particular plan of action. The third assignment is to express personal opinions: students explain what an individual's responsibility to society is.

In addition, there is a **nonfiction reading assignment**. Students are required to read a piece of nonfiction related in some way to The Pigman. After reading their nonfiction pieces, students will fill out a worksheet on which they answer questions regarding facts, interpretation, criticism, and personal opinions. During one class period, students make oral presentations about the nonfiction pieces they have read. This not only exposes all students to a wealth of information, it also gives students the opportunity to practice public speaking.

The **review lesson** pulls together all of the aspects of the unit. The teacher is given four or five choices of activities or games to use which all serve the same basic function of reviewing all of the information presented in the unit.

The **unit test** comes in two formats: multiple choice or short answer. As a convenience, two different tests for each format have been included. There is also an advanced short answer unit test for upper level students.

In a **project assignment,** students must give a five minute presentation in which they describe and briefly demonstrate their hobbies.

There are additional **support materials** included with this unit. The **extra activities section** includes suggestions for an in-class library, crossword and word search puzzles related to the novel, and extra vocabulary worksheets. There is a list of **bulletin board ideas** which gives the teacher suggestions for bulletin boards to go along with this unit. In addition, there is a list of **extra class activities** the teacher could choose from to enhance the unit or as a substitution for an exercise the teacher might feel is inappropriate for his/her class. **Answer keys** are located directly after the **reproducible student materials** throughout the unit. The student materials may be reproduced for use in the teacher's classroom without infringement of copyrights. No other portion of this unit may be reproduced without the written consent of Teacher's Pet Publications, Inc.

The **level** of this unit can be varied depending upon the criteria on which the individual assignments are graded, the teacher's expectations of his/her students in class discussions, and the formats chosen for the study guides, quizzes and test. If teachers have other ideas/activities they wish to use, they can usually easily be inserted prior to the review lesson.

UNIT OBJECTIVES - *The Pigman*

1. Students will discuss the ideas of death/life, lying/truth, and individualism/conformity as well as the roles of parents, friends and others in our lives.

2. Students will demonstrate their understanding of the text on four levels: factual, interpretive, critical and personal.

3. Students will define their own viewpoints on the aforementioned themes.

4. Students will learn about many different hobbies, constructive things they can do in their spare time.

5. Students will study the character development of John and Lorraine as they learn about life.

6. Students will be given the opportunity to practice reading aloud and silently to improve their skills in each area.

7. Students will answer questions to demonstrate their knowledge and understanding of the main events and characters in *The Pigman* as they relate to the author's theme development.

8. Students will enrich their vocabularies and improve their understanding of the novel through the vocabulary lessons prepared for use in conjunction with the novel.

9. The writing assignments in this unit are geared to several purposes:
    a. To have students demonstrate their abilities to inform, to persuade, or to express their own personal ideas
        Note: Students will demonstrate ability to write effectively to <u>inform</u> by developing and organizing facts to convey information. Students will demonstrate the ability to write effectively to <u>persuade</u> by selecting and organizing relevant information, establishing an argumentative purpose, and by designing an appropriate strategy for an identified audience. Students will demonstrate the ability to write effectively to <u>express personal ideas</u> by selecting a form and its appropriate elements.
    b. To check the students' reading comprehension
    c. To make students think about the ideas presented by the novel
    d. To encourage logical thinking
    e. To provide an opportunity to practice good grammar and improve students' use of the English language.

READING ASSIGNMENT SHEET - *The Pigman*

Date Assigned	Chapters Assigned	Completion Date
	1-2	
	3-6	
	7-9	
	10-12	
	13-15	

UNIT OUTLINE - *The Pigman*

1 Introduction PV 1-2	2 Read 1-2 PV 3-6	3 Study ?s 1-2 Read 3-6 PVR 7-9	4 Library	5 Study ?s 3-6, 7-9 PVR 10-12
6 Study ?s 10-12 Writing Assignment 1 PVR 13-15	7 Study ?s 13-15 Vocabulary	8 Extra Discussion ?s	9 Quotations	10 Writing Assignment 2
11 Group Activity	12 Reports & Discussion	13 Project Presentations	14 Project Presentations	15 Writing Assignment 3
16 Review	17 Test			

Key: P = Preview Study Questions   V = Vocabulary Prereading Worksheets   R = Read

STUDY GUIDE QUESTIONS

SHORT ANSWER STUDY GUIDE QUESTIONS - *The Pigman*

Chapters 1 - 4
1. Compare and contrast John and Lorraine.
2. What was a "telephone marathon"?
3. Who are Dennis and Norton?
4. How did Lorraine and John first encounter Mr. Pignati?
5. What was odd about their phone conversation with Mr. Pignati?
6. Why did Lorraine and John go to Mr. Pignati's house?

Chapters 5 & 6
1. Why did John lie to Dennis and Norton about the phone call to Mr. Pignati?
2. Describe Mr. Pignati.
3. What did Mr. Pignati do to lengthen Lorraine and John's first visit? Why?
4. Why did Lorraine and John call Mr. Pignati The Pigman?
5. Contrast Lorraine and John's attitudes towards taking Mr. Pignati's $10.
6. Lorraine says her mother has a "real hang-up about men and boys." What does her mother constantly tell her?
7. What kind of a person is Lorraine's mother?
8. Who is the Bore?
9. What "omens" did Lorraine encounter at the zoo?
10. Who is Bobo?
11. What got Bobo, two chimps and the gorilla all worked up into a tizzy?

Chapters 7 - 9
1. Why do the kids go to Masterson's Tomb?
2. Why does John say he thinks he is really looking for a ghost?
3. How does John's father want him to spend his spare time?
4. Why does John's father say, "Thank God Kenneth isn't a lunatic"?
5. What do we learn about John's father when he says, "Be yourself! Be individualistic!"
6. What did John find out about Conchetta?
7. What does Mr. Pignati buy for Lorraine and John?
8. Why does Norton threaten to go to Mr. Pignati's house?
9. Why did John "know" he would kill Norton if he hurt Mr. Pignati?

The Pigman Study Guide Questions Page Two

Chapters 10 - 12
1. What lies had Lorraine been telling her mother?
2. How do we know Lorraine's mother is suspicious? How does Lorraine keep getting away with her lies?
3. Why was Mr. Pignati so sad that Sunday night in January?
4. Why did John and Lorraine confess that they were not charity workers?
5. What confession did Mr. Pignati make?
6. Why were Mr. Pignati, Lorraine and John skating in the house?
7. What happened to Mr. Pignati?
8. John and Lorraine tell the police that they are Pignati's children. Why?
9. Mr. Pignati told the kids to take care of what two things until he returned?
10. What happened to John and Lorraine's relationship in the period following Mr. Pignati's heart attack?
11. What did Lorraine's nightmare foreshadow?
12. What was John's idea for Friday night (the night before Pigman would be home)?

Chapters 13 - 15
1. Describe the party.
2. What happened when Norton arrived?
3. Who came in just before John passed out?
4. How did Lorraine's mother react when she found out about Lorraine's escapades?
5. How did John's parents react when they found out about his escapades?
6. Why did the kids want to take Mr. Pignati to the zoo?
7. What happened when they got to the zoo?
8. Why did Lorraine and John leave the Pigman?

ANSWER KEY: SHORT ANSWER STUDY GUIDE QUESTIONS - *The Pigman*

Chapters 1 - 4
1. Compare and contrast John and Lorraine.
   John hates school and is a rebel. He set off bombs in the bathroom, staged fruit rolls, cursed and wrote on desks. Lorraine is not so much a rebel; she doesn't do the destructive or disruptive things that John does. She is more of an analyst. Neither John nor Lorraine has a perfect home life; their parents are shown as real people with problems of their own.

2. What was a "telephone marathon"?
   John, Lorraine, and their friends would call numbers at random from the phone book and see how long they could keep the person they called on the line.

3. Who are Dennis and Norton?
   They are "friends" of Lorraine and John. They don't like each other. Norton has a habit of shoplifting. The telephone marathons take place at Dennis' house.

4. How did Lorraine and John first encounter Mr. Pignati?
   Lorraine picked his number from the phone book for a telephone marathon.

5. What was odd about their phone conversation with Mr. Pignati?
   Mr. Pignati kept making jokes and seemed to want to talk to them.

6. Why did Lorraine and John go to Mr. Pignati's house?
   They went to collect the $10 for the L & J Fund.

Chapters 5 & 6
1. Why did John lie to Dennis and Norton about the phone call to Mr. Pignati?
   He didn't want them (esp. Norton) to "hustle in on the deal" or "take advantage of the old man."

2. Describe Mr. Pignati.
   He was in his late 50's, was "pretty big," and he had a bit of a beer stomach. The thing that really impressed John was Mr. Pignati's huge smile.

3. What did Mr. Pignati do to lengthen Lorraine and John's first visit? Why?
   First he told them about the memory trick, then invited them to go to the zoo, and then showed them the pig collection.

4. Why did Lorraine and John call Mr. Pignati The Pigman?
    They called him that because of the pig collection he had started for his wife, to remind her of him -- <u>Pignati</u>.

5. Contrast Lorraine and John's attitudes towards taking Mr. Pignati's $10.
    John was for it; Lorraine was against it.

6. Lorraine says her mother has a "real hang-up about men and boys." What does her mother constantly tell her?
    She constantly told Lorraine to look out for boys and men, that they only want one thing.

7. What kind of a person is Lorraine's mother?
    Lorraine's mother has troubles of her own. She has "hang-ups" (as Lorraine calls it) about men because her husband ran out on her. She is not especially ethical; she steals and takes money from the mortuary. She often makes Lorraine feel guilty, and she doesn't seem to value school.

8. Who is the Bore?
    John's father is "the Bore."

9. What "omens" did Lorraine encounter at the zoo?
    She mentioned the lady with the peanuts, an attack by a peacock, and the child at the nocturnal room.

10. Who is Bobo?
    He is an ugly, vicious baboon Mr. Pignati has befriended.

11. What got Bobo, two chimps and the gorilla all worked up into a tizzy?
    John, Lorraine and Mr. Pignati were making monkey noises. (Uggauggaboo!)

<u>Chapters 7 - 9</u>
1. Why do the kids go to Masterson's Tomb?
    They hang out there and drink beer.

2. Why does John say he thinks he is really looking for a ghost?
    He is looking for "anything to prove that when [he] drops dead there's a chance [he'll] be doing something a little more exciting than decaying."

3. How does John's father want him to spend his spare time?
    He wants John to work at the Exchange with him a few days a week after school.

4. Why does John's father say, "Thank God Kenneth isn't a lunatic"?
    He has found out that John wants to be an actor and has no interest in the Exchange or the lifestyle that goes with it.

5. What do we learn about John's father when he says, "Be yourself! Be individualistic! . . . But for God's sake get your hair cut. You look like an oddball."
    He misses the point totally that perhaps John's long hair is an outward sign of his individuality. He wants John to be an individual but within conventional standards.

6. What did John find out about Conchetta?
    She is dead, not visiting in California.

7. What does Mr. Pignati buy for Lorraine and John?
    He buys "delicacies" (frog legs, chocolate covered ants, fish killies), nylon stockings, and roller skates.

8. Why does Norton threaten to go to Mr. Pignati's house?
    He is insulted that he wasn't invited from the start. He wants to know what Pignati has worth stealing.

9. Why did John "know" he would kill Norton if he hurt Mr. Pignati?
    The Pigman was the best influence on his life at this point in time. He had grown very fond of Mr. Pignati.

Chapters 10 - 12

1. What lies had Lorraine been telling her mother?
    She said she wasn't in the car her mother had seen, that she had been at Latin Club and had missed the bus, and that she had paid for the stockings with money she had saved by not riding the bus and by skipping lunches.

2. How do we know Lorraine's mother is suspicious? How does Lorraine keep getting away with her lies?
    She asks where Lorraine has been, looks for her reaction to questions, and asks the same questions again later to compare the answers. Lorraine's mother is busy working and too tired and rushed to do a thorough investigation -- and Lorraine's answers sound reasonable.

3. Why was Mr. Pignati so sad that Sunday night in January?
    He was sad because Bobo wouldn't eat; Mr. Pignati realized that Bobo was getting old. He was especially depressed because it was his anniversary, and he was missing his wife.

4. Why did John and Lorraine confess that they were not charity workers?
    They felt guilty about lying to Mr. Pignati.

5. What confession did Mr. Pignati make?
   That his wife was actually dead, not in California.

6. Why were Mr. Pignati, Lorraine and John skating in the house?
   They were having fun, trying to cheer up Mr. Pignati.

7. What happened to Mr. Pignati?
   He had a heart attack.

8. John and Lorraine tell the police that they are Pignati's children. Why?
   They know that that's the only way they'll get any information, and they really do feel like his children.

9. Mr. Pignati told the kids to take care of what two things until he returned?
   He wanted them to take care of Bobo and his house.

10. What happened to John and Lorraine's relationship in the period following Mr. Pignati's heart attack?
    They began to realize that they cared for each other as more than just friends. In the days that followed, they wanted to have the same nice time as Monday evening but things just didn't work out. They began feeling awkward around each other.

11. What did Lorraine's nightmare foreshadow?
    It foreshadowed The Pigman's death.

12. What was John's idea for Friday night (the night before Pigman would be home)?
    He wanted to have a quiet drink with some friends, to have a little party.

Chapters 13 - 15
1. Describe the party.
   The party was okay at first, but it didn't go as planned. There were more people than "a few friends," and after some drinks, everyone started getting too carried away and reckless. Things got ruined.

2. What happened when Norton arrived?
   He and John got into an argument. Norton stole the oscilloscope and broke up Mr. Pignati's pigs.

3. Who came in just before John passed out?
   Mr. Pignati came in.

4. How did Lorraine's mother react when she found out about Lorraine's escapades?
   First she was angry and hit Lorraine. Then they sat down and talked things over in a reasonable way. Then she had doubts again and returned to her old questions and warnings about men.

5. How did John's parents react when they found out about his escapades?
   He said they looked tired and old. They decided to send him to a psychiatrist.

6. Why did the kids want to take Mr. Pignati to the zoo?
   They wanted to help make up for the mess they caused and wanted him to feel better.

7. What happened when they got to the zoo?
   They found out Bobo had died last week. Mr. Pignati had another attack and died.

8. Why did Lorraine and John leave the Pigman?
   They were already in trouble, and there was nothing they could to for Mr. Pignati.

MULTIPLE CHOICE STUDY GUIDE/QUIZ QUESTIONS - *The Pigman*

Chapters 1-4

1. Which statement best describes John and Lorraine?
    A. John is depressed and lethargic. Lorraine is destructive and violent.
    B. John is destructive and rebellious. Lorraine is analytic and conforming.
    C. John is friendly and creative. Lorraine is intelligent and shy.
    D. John is a model student. Lorraine hates school.

2. What did John, Lorraine, and their friends do when they had a "telephone marathon?"
    A. They made phone calls to raise money for the school band.
    B. They kept track of times to see which boyfriend and girlfriend could spend the most time on the telephone together in a week
    C. They called numbers at random from a phone book to see how long they could keep the person they called on the line.
    D. They counted to see how many friends could talk to each other during one conversation.

3. Identify Dennis and Norton.
    A. Dennis sets bombs in the school bathroom. Norton is Mr. Pignati's grandson.
    B. Dennis holds the telephone marathons at his house. Norton is a shoplifter.
    C. Dennis is romantically interested in Lorraine. Norton curses in school.
    D. Dennis is a "goody-goody." Norton started the phone marathon.

4. How did Lorraine and John first encounter Mr. Pignati?
    A. They met him on a trip to the zoo.
    B. Lorraine's mother was nursing him and told Lorraine about him.
    C. He gave a talk at their school
    D. Lorraine picked his number from the telephone book for a marathon.

5. What was odd about their first conversation with Mr. Pignati?
    A. They thought he was taping it.
    B. He was speaking Italian even though they spoke to him in English.
    C. He made jokes and seemed to want to talk to them.
    D. They used the speaker phone so the others could listen in.

6. Why did Lorraine and John go to Mr. Pignati's house?
    A. He asked them to do some odd jobs.
    B. They went to collect the money for the L& J Fund.
    C. They wanted to see what he looked like.
    D. They were going to set him up for a robbery.

The Pigman Multiple Choice Study Questions Page 2

<u>Chapters 5 - 6</u>

7. Why did John lie to Dennis and Norton about the phone call to Mr. Pignati?
    A. He thought Dennis and Norton would make fun of him.
    B. He was embarrassed that Lorraine had talked longer than he ever had.
    C. He didn't want to give away his secrets of success.
    D. He didn't want them to hustle in on the deal or take advantage of the old man.

8. Which does not describe Mr. Pignati?
    A. Full beard and moustache
    B. Late 50's
    C. Pretty large, beer stomach
    D. Huge smile

9. What did Mr. Pignati do to lengthen John and Lorraine's first visit?
    A. He played the guitar for them.
    B. He offered to pay them to stay and do some jobs around the house.
    C. He did a memory trick, invited them to go to the zoo, and showed them his pig collection.
    D. He took them for a ride in his new car. Then he let each of them drive it.

10. Why did Lorraine and John call Mr. Pignati "The Pigman?"
    A. He had started a pig collection for his wife to remind her of him.
    B. He told them he was a pig farmer before he retired.
    C. They had a secret code and identified people by animal names.
    D. He was "piggy" about taking up a lot of their time.

11. What were Lorraine's and John's attitudes towards taking Mr. Pignati's $10.
    A. They both wanted to take the money.
    B. John wanted to take the money, but Lorraine didn't
    C. Neither of them wanted to go through with it.
    D. Lorraine wanted to take the money, but John didn't.

The Pigman Multiple Choice Study Questions Page 3

12. Lorraine says her mother has a "real hang-up about men and boys." What does her mother constantly tell her?
    A. Rich men are smarter; never go out with a poor man.
    B. Look for older men because they are more mature.
    C. Most men drink too much.
    D. Men only want one thing.

13. Which does not describe Lorraine's mother?
    A. Steals food and money from clients
    B. Alcoholic
    C. Angry because her husband left her
    D. Doesn't value school

14. Who is the Bore?
    A. John's father
    B. Mr. Pignati when he starts telling jokes
    C. John and Lorraine's English teacher
    D. The first pig in Mr. Pignati's collection

15. What "omens" did Lorraine encounter at the zoo?
    A. An angry zookeeper, a dead turtle, and a stalled touring car
    B. Lights on in the nocturnal room and an increase in the admission price
    C. A lady with peanuts, an attack by a peacock, and a child at the nocturnal room
    D. A late arrival, seeing Lorraine's cousin and her children, and wheezing from the smell in the monkey house

16. Who is Bobo?
    A. John's little brother
    B. An ugly, vicious baboon
    C. Mr. Pignati's wife
    D. One of Norton's friends

17. What got Bobo, two chimps, and the gorilla all worked up into a tizzy?
    A. John and Lorraine were feeding them peanuts.
    B. Mr. Pignati was singing to them in Italian.
    C. John threw a ball into the cage.
    D. John, Lorraine, and Mr. Pignati were making monkey noises.

The Pigman Multiple Choice Study Questions Page 4

Chapters 7-9

18. Why do the kids go to Masterson's Tomb?
    A. They hang out and drink beer there.
    B. Norton bet them $10 each they wouldn't do it.
    C. It was part of the initiation into their club.
    D. They were looking for money that was said to be buried there.

19. Why does John say he thinks he is really looking for a ghost?
    A. He wants to test his courage.
    B. He is showing off his bravery to Lorraine.
    C. He will do anything to prove there is an afterlife.
    D. He thinks he can communicate with it.

20. How does John's father want him to spend his spare time?
    A. Taking extra music lessons
    B. Helping his mother around the house
    C. Working at the Exchange
    D. Doing community volunteer service

21. What is John's father's reaction to John's telling him he wants to be an actor?
    A. "Thank God Kenneth isn't a lunatic."
    B. "Don't worry about that."
    C. "Are you going to have dessert?"
    D. "I want you to be your own man."

22. What do we learn about John's father when he says, "Be yourself! Be individualistic! But for God's sake get your hair cut. You look like an oddball."
    A. He has a strange sense of humor.
    B. He says what he thinks people want to hear.
    C. He hates the thought of John being an actor and will do anything to stop him.
    D. He wants John to be an individual but to stay within conventional standards.

23. What did John find out about Conchetta?
    A. She moved to California for good, not just a visit.
    B. She is dead.
    C. She was never real; she was in Mr. Pignati's imagination.
    D. She had divorced him years ago.

The Pigman Multiple Choice Study Questions Page 5

24. What does Mr. Pignati buy for Lorraine and John?
    A. Records, beer, and cigarettes
    B. Clothes and jewelry
    C. Pet monkeys
    D. Food delicacies, nylon stockings, and roller skates

25. Why does Norton threaten to go to Mr. Pignati's house?
    A. He thinks Mr. Pignati deserves to know the truth about John and Lorraine.
    B. He wants to convince Mr. Pignati to buy things for him instead of for Lorraine and John.
    C. He wants to see what Mr. Pignati has that is worth stealing.
    D. He wants to talk the other kids into leaving the party early.

26. Why did John "know" he would kill Norton if he hurt Mr. Pignati?
    A. John was fond of him, and Mr. Pignati had been a good influence.
    B. John didn't want to be blamed if anything happened.
    C. John was looking for any excuse to get at Norton.
    D. John knew he had a good thing going. He didn't want Norton to spoil it.

The Pigman Multiple Choice Study Questions Page 6

Chapters 10-12

27. What lies had Lorraine been telling her mother?
    A. She was working on the school newspaper, a friend gave her the stockings, and there was another girl at school who looked like her and was the one in the car.
    B. She was doing housecleaning after school to help out. One of her employers had picked her up from school. That person also gave her the stockings.
    C. She had been volunteering at the zoo. A friend had given her the ride to the zoo. She found the stockings in a bag on a bench there.
    D. She wasn't in the car. She had been at Latin Club and had missed the bus. She paid for the stockings by not riding the bus and skipping lunches.

28. How do we know Lorraine's mother is suspicious? How does Lorraine keep getting away with her lies?
    A. She calls Lorraine's friends to check on the story, and they lie for her.
    B. She looks for Lorraine's reaction to questions and asks the same questions later to compare answers. Lorraine's answers sound reasonable, and her mother is too busy to check further.
    C. She talks to the school guidance counselor, who then meets with Lorraine. Lorraine tells the counselor the same lies she told her mother, and there is no way to prove whether or not she is telling the truth.
    D. She asks Lorraine for the name and phone number of the moderator of the Latin Club. Lorraine gives her the name of a friend who has agreed to cover for her.

29. Why was Mr. Pignati so sad that Sunday night in January?
    A. He thought John and Lorraine didn't want to be his friends anymore.
    B. He knew he was getting too old to live by himself.
    C. He realized that Bobo was getting old. It was also his anniversary, and he missed his wife.
    D. He wanted to go to California to see his sister, but she didn't want to see him.

30. What did John and Lorraine's guilt prompt them to do?
    A. Clean Mr. Pignati's house thoroughly.
    B. Tell the truth about being charity workers.
    C. Stop seeing Mr. Pignati.
    D. Give back the money.

31. What confession did Mr. Pignati make?
    A. His wife was dead, not in California.
    B. He knew all along they were lying to him.
    C. He only had a few months to live.
    D. He had been in prison when he was younger.

The Pigman Multiple Choice Study Questions Page 7

32. Why were Mr. Pignati, Lorraine, and John skating in the house?
    A. Mr. Pignati had never skated before and was afraid to go outside.
    B. They were all drunk and didn't really know what they were doing.
    C. John and Lorraine didn't want any one to see them with Mr. Pignati.
    D. They were having fun, trying to cheer Mr. Pignati up.

33. What happened to Mr. Pignati?
    A. He tripped and broke his leg.
    B. He beat John to the top of the stairs and his sorrow left him.
    C. He had a heart attack.
    D. He lost his balance and crashed into the pig collection, breaking most of them.

34. John and Lorraine want to get information about Mr. Pignati. What do they tell the police?
    A. They are social workers assigned to his case.
    B. They are his only friends.
    C. He is one of Lorraine's mother's patients, and they have been helping out.
    D. They are his children.

35. What did Mr. Pignati ask them to do while he was in the hospital?
    A. Bring him some chocolate covered ants and frogs legs.
    B. Take care of Bobo and the house.
    C. Call the church and ask the priest to come to see him.
    D. Cut school to visit him because he was afraid of being alone.

36. What happened to John and Lorraine's relationship in the period following Mr. Pignati's heart attack?
    A. They realized they cared for each other as more than friends, and they began feeling awkward around each other.
    B. They became jealous of each other, and each wanted all of Mr. Pignati's attention.
    C. They realized they were seeing too much of each other and cut back on the time they were spending together.
    D. Lorraine stopped talking to John because she blamed him for causing the heart attack.

37. What did Lorraine's nightmare foreshadow?
    A. The end of her friendship with John
    B. The damage to Mr. Pignati's house
    C. Mr. Pignati's death
    D. Her mother's discovering the truth and punishing her

The Pigman Multiple Choice Study Questions Page 9

38. What was John's idea for Friday night (the night before Mr. Pignati would be home)?
    A. Spend the evening at the hospital with Mr. Pignati
    B. Clean Mr. Pignati's whole house
    C. Have a little party, a quiet drink with some friends
    D. Talk to Lorraine about their relationship

The Pigman Multiple Choice Study Questions Page 10

Chapters 13-15

39. Describe the party.
    A. It didn't go as planned. Too many people came, and they got reckless and ruined things.
    B. It was a flop. Most of their friends boycotted because Norton wasn't invited.
    C. It was mild and quiet, just as planned.
    D. John and Lorraine felt guilty. They turned everyone away at the door.

40. What happened when Norton arrived?
    A. John hit him and threw him out.
    B. Lorraine distracted him by introducing him to one of her girlfriends.
    C. He and John made up. He stayed on his best behavior.
    D. He stole the oscilloscope and broke up the pigs.

41. Who came in just before John passed out?
    A. John's father
    B. Lorraine's mother
    C. Mr. Pignati
    D. Kenneth

42. How did Lorraine's mother react when she found out about Lorraine's escapades?
    A. She told Lorraine she was as bad as her father and threw her out of the house permanently.
    B. First she was angry and hit Lorraine. Then they talked reasonably. Then she returned to her old questions and warnings about men.
    C. She was furious. She asked the policemen to take Lorraine to a juvenile detention center.
    D. She became hysterical and started beating Lorraine. The police had to restrain her.

43. How did John's parents react when they found out about his escapades?
    A. They said he looked tired and old. They decided to send him to a psychiatrist.
    B. They made arrangements for John to go and live with an uncle in another state.
    C. They blamed everything on Lorraine and said he couldn't see her again.
    D. They said he would have to work at the Exchange every day to earn enough to repay Mr. Pignati for all of the damage.

The Pigman Multiple Choice Study Questions Page 11

44. What did John and Lorraine do to make up for the trouble they caused Mr. Pignati?
    A. They got all of their friends to help repair the house.
    B. They bought new pigs.
    C. They took Mr. Pignati to the zoo.
    D. They wrote a letter of apology.

45. What happened when they got to the zoo? What was Mr. Pignati's reaction?
    A. Bobo had been moved to another zoo. Mr. Pignati was glad.
    B. Bobo and Mr. Pignati were reunited and happy.
    C. The monkey house was closed. Mr. Pignati lost his temper and insisted on being let in. They were asked to leave the zoo.
    D. Bobo was dead. Mr. Pignati had a heart attack and died.

46. Why did Lorraine and John leave the Pigman?
    A. They went to get help.
    B. They were already in trouble and there was nothing more they could do.
    C. They were glad to be rid of him.
    D. They were afraid they would be accused of murder.

ANSWER KEY - MULTIPLE CHOICE STUDY/QUIZ QUESTIONS
The Pigman

Chapters 1 - 4
1. A
2. C
3. B
4. D
5. C
6. B

Chapters 5 & 6
7. D
8. A
9. C
10. A
11. B
12. D
13. B
14. A
15. C
16. B
17. D

Chapters 7, 8 & 9
18. A
19. C
20. C
21. A
22. D
23. B
24. D
25. C
26. A

Chapters 10, 11, & 12
27. D
28. B
29. C
30. B
31. A
32. D
33. C
34. D
35. B
36. A
37. C
38. C

Chapters 13, 14, & 15
39. A
40. D
41. C
42. C
43. B
44. C
45. D
46. B

PREREADING VOCABULARY WORKSHEETS

VOCABULARY - *The Pigman*

<u>Chapters 1 - 2</u>: Part I: Using Prior Knowledge and Contextual Clues

Below are the sentences in which the vocabulary words appear in the text. Read the sentence. Use any clues you can find in the sentence combined with your prior knowledge, and write what you think the underlined words mean on the lines provided.

1. . . . a whole flock of <u>gestapo</u> would race in there and blame them. sure they didn't do it, but it's pretty hard to say you're innocent when you're caught with a lung full of rich, mellow tobacco smoke.

   _____

2. After my bomb <u>avocation</u>, I became the organizer of the supercolossal fruit roll.

   _____

3. We were supposed to study <u>incandescent</u> lamps, but he spent the period telling us about commemorative stamps.

   _____

4. I'm not panting, and I'm not about to have a <u>thrombosis</u>.

   _____

5. I've spent hours trying to <u>analyze</u> the situation, and the closest I've been able to come to a theory is that his father set a bad example . . . .

   _____

6. . . . I thought for sure he was laughing at me. . . . They call that <u>paranoia</u>.

   _____

7. I was <u>mortified</u> picking it up because it fell between the seat and the window, and I was sure I'd look like an enormous cow bending over to get it.

   _____

Vocabulary - *The Pigman* Chapters 1 - 2 Continued

Part II: Determining the Meaning

You have tried to figure out the meanings of the vocabulary words for Chapters 1 - 2. Now match the vocabulary words to their dictionary definitions. If there are words for which you cannot figure out the definition by contextual clues and by process of elimination, look them up in a dictionary.

___ 1. gestapo   A. examine methodically
___ 2. avocation   B. police organization that uses terroristic methods
___ 3. incandescent   C. humiliated; embarrassed
___ 4. thrombosis   D. hobby; work; profession
___ 5. analyze   E. extreme, irrational distrust of others
___ 6. paranoia   F. giving visible light as a result of being heated
___ 7. mortified   G. presence of a clot in a blood vessel

Vocabulary - *The Pigman* Chapters 3 - 6

Part I: Using Prior Knowledge and Contextual Clues

Below are the sentences in which the vocabulary words appear in the text. Read the sentence. Use any clues you can find in the sentence combined with your prior knowledge, and write what you think the underlined words mean on the lines provided.

1. I suppose it all started when Lorraine and I and these two <u>amoebae</u> called Dennis Kobin and Norton Kelly were hot on these phone gags . . . .

_____

2. When he started another joke I looked at John's face and began to realize it was he who had started me telling all these <u>prevarications</u>.

_____

3. It's what they call a <u>compensation</u> syndrome. His own life is so boring when measured against his daydreams that he can't stand it, so he makes up things to pretend it's exciting.

_____

4. It's a kind of subconscious <u>schizophrenic</u> fibbing.

_____

5. We can tell him the L & J Fund is intended to <u>subsidize</u> writers and actors if you want.

_____

6. He could've been some psycho with an electric carving knife who'd <u>dismember</u> our bodies and wouldn't get caught until our teeth clogged up the sewer . . . .

_____

7. I mean, that's how <u>antagonistic</u> she was. A real devoted antagonist. You could tell she hated kids---just hated them.

_____

Vocabulary - *The Pigman* Chapters 3 - 6 Continued

Part II: Determining the Meaning

You have tried to figure out the meanings of the vocabulary words for Chapters 3 - 6. Now match the vocabulary words to their dictionary definitions. If there are words for which you cannot figure out the definition by contextual clues and by process of elimination, look them up in a dictionary.

___ 8. amoebae
___ 9. prevarications
___ 10. compensation
___ 11. schizophrenic
___ 12. subsidize
___ 13. dismember
___ 14. antagonistic

A. lies; statements straying from the truth
B. divide into pieces
C. a microscopic animal found in water, soil, and as a parasite in other animals
D. saying or doing things to intentionally annoy or displease someone
E. offset; counterbalance; substitution
F. give financial assistance to
G. psychological disorder

Vocabulary - *The Pigman* - Chapters 7, 8 & 9

Part I: Using Prior Knowledge and Contextual Clues
    Below are the sentences in which the vocabulary words appear in the text. Read the sentence. Use any clues you can find in the sentence combined with your prior knowledge, and write what you think the underlined words mean on the lines provided.

1. If you let her, Lorraine would eat until she dropped, and if she keeps going at that rate, I'm afraid she's going to be somewhat more than voluptuous. She could end up just plain fat.

_____

2. Maybe one of the molecules of iron from the corpse's hemoglobin is in the strand of grass next to my ear. But the embalmers drain all the blood--well probably not *every* drop.

_____

3. Don't give the ingrate anything.

_____

4. All it had was this big desk . . . and a big oscilloscope, with its guts hanging out . . . .

_____

5. There was enough artillery in Beekman's toy department to wipe out Red China and the Mau-Mau tribe of Africa . . . .

_____

6. But the kids used to make cracks about him, so that made him go berserk around the age of ten.

_____

7. It's like paranoia in reverse when people are really calling you insulting things and you deliberately pretend they aren't.

_____

Vocabulary - *The Pigman* Chapters 7-9

Part II: Determining the Meaning

You have tried to figure out the meanings of the vocabulary words for Chapters 7 - 9. Now match the vocabulary words to their dictionary definitions. If there are words for which you cannot figure out the definition by contextual clues and by process of elimination, look them up in a dictionary.

___ 15. voluptuous   A. electronic instrument that shows movements of voltage and electronic currents
___ 16. hemoglobin   B. iron-containing respiratory pigment in red blood cells
___ 17. ingrate   C. mentally or emotionally upset; deranged
___ 18. oscilloscope   D. intentionally; on purpose
___ 19. artillery   E. an ungrateful person
___ 20. berserk   F. large caliber weapons
___ 21. deliberately   G. giving ample, unrestrained pleasure to the senses

Vocabulary - *The Pigman* Chapters 10, 11 & 12

Part I: Using Prior Knowledge and Contextual Clues

Below are the sentences in which the vocabulary words appear in the text. Read the sentence. Use any clues you can find in the sentence combined with your prior knowledge, and write what you think the underlined words mean on the lines provided.

1. She never talks about him now--just how awful men are in general. She's what the psychologists call fixated on the subject.

_____

2. She mulled that over a few seconds, but she had to get to work on time and couldn't devote her full energies to interrogating.

_____

3. The wife runs back to the LOVER's house and explains to him what her predicament is and asks him for fifty cents to pay the BOATMAN.

_____

4. . . . there weren't many obstacles you could skate around on the ground floor except the kitchen table, and that got mundane after awhile.

_____

5. I don't like spaghetti when it's normal, let alone congealed.

_____

6. If I didn't know how maladjusted John is at times, I would have simply walked out of that house and not spoken to him again as long as I lived.

_____

7. Just a few intimate friends for a quiet little drink.

_____

Vocabulary - *The Pigman* Chapters 10-12

Part II: Determining the Meaning
You have tried to figure out the meanings of the vocabulary words for Chapters 10, 11, & 12. Now match the vocabulary words to their dictionary definitions. If there are words for which you cannot figure out the definition by contextual clues and by process of elimination, look them up in a dictionary.

___ 22. fixated   A. ordinary; boring
___ 23. mulled   B. close; personal
___ 24. predicament   C. to become overly concerned with one subject
___ 25. mundane   D. stuck together; jelled; solidified
___ 26. congealed   E. not able to adjust to the demands of personal relationships
___ 27. maladjusted   F. troublesome situation
___ 28. intimate   G. thought about; pondered

Vocabulary - *The Pigman* - Chapters 13, 14 & 15

Part I: Using Prior Knowledge and Contextual Clues
 Below are the sentences in which the vocabulary words appear in the text. Read the sentence. Use any clues you can find in the sentence combined with your prior knowledge, and write what you think the underlined words mean on the lines provided.

1. She's got a lovely voice, but her memory is like that of a titmouse with curvature of the brain.

_____

2. He was so much taller and thinner than the other one that the two of them together looked rather incongruous.

_____

3. "He's out for the night," the fat cop said, adjusting his hat.

_____

4. She was sitting at the kitchen table, crying--a slightly exaggerated crying which seemed to make our relationship even more artificial.

_____

5. There were a few moments of minor relapses, like when I told her I had never belonged to the Latin Club, but on the whole she took things better than I thought she would.

_____

6. One of the attendants was washing the sea-lion manure off the middle platform of the pool, and at least he was able to do that with a certain degree of proficiency.

_____

7. I stayed until the ambulance doctor gestured that the Pigman was dead.

_____

8. The police and attendants moved calmly, surely, as if they were performing a ritual and had forgotten the meaning of it.

_____

Vocabulary - *The Pigman* Chapters 13-15

Part II: Determining the Meaning
     You have tried to figure out the meanings of the vocabulary words for Chapters 13 - 15. Now match the vocabulary words to their dictionary definitions. If there are words for which you cannot figure out the definition by contextual clues and by process of elimination, look them up in a dictionary.

___ 29. titmouse	A. fixing to a more compatible position
___ 30. incongruous	B. motioned with hands
___ 31. adjusting	C. competency; ability to do something well
___ 32. exaggerated	D. small insect-eating bird
___ 33. relapses	E. ceremony; routine
___ 34. proficiency	F. falling back to a former condition
___ 35. gestured	G. enlarged or increased to an abnormal degree
___ 36. ritual	H. incompatible; not belonging together

ANSWER KEY - VOCABULARY
The Pigman

Chapters 1 - 2
1. B
2. D
3. F
4. G
5. A
6. E
7. C

Chapters 3 - 6
8. C
9. A
10. E
11. G
12. F
13. B
14. D

Chapters 7 - 9
15. G
16. B
17. E
18. A
19. F
20. C
21. D

Chapters 10 - 12
22. C
23. G
24. F
25. A
26. D
27. E
28. B

Chapters 13 - 15
29. D
30. H
31. A
32. G
33. F
34. C
35. B
36. E

DAILY LESSONS

LESSON ONE

Objectives
1. To introduce *The Pigman* unit
2. To distribute books and other related materials
3. To preview the study questions for chapters 1-2
4. To familiarize students with the vocabulary for chapters 1-2

NOTE: Prior to this lesson, students should have been assigned to bring in some thing (or a picture or representative item) important to them in their lives. It can be anything that can be stapled or tacked to the bulletin board. It should be something that won't be missed if it is stolen from the bulletin board if you live in an area where that would be a consideration.

Activity #1
Ask students one by one to show or describe the things they brought to represent something important in their lives and to explain the significance. After each student finishes explaining his item, he/she should staple it up on the bulletin board you have prepared titled, THE PIGMAN: WHAT IS IMPORTANT IN LIFE? Let students write their names next to the things they post on the board if they want to.

Activity #2
Distribute the materials students will use in this unit. Explain in detail how students are to use these materials.

Study Guides Students should read the study guide questions for each reading assignment prior to beginning the reading assignment to get a feeling for what events and ideas are important in the section they are about to read. After reading the section, students will (as a class or individually) answer the questions to review the important events and ideas from that section of the book. Students should keep the study guides as study materials for the unit test.

Vocabulary Prior to reading a reading assignment, students will do vocabulary work related to the section of the book they are about to read. Following the completion of the reading of the book, there will be a vocabulary review of all the words used in the vocabulary assignments. Students should keep their vocabulary work as study materials for the unit test.

Reading Assignment Sheet You need to fill in the reading assignment sheet to let students know by when their reading has to be completed. You can either write the assignment sheet up on a side blackboard or bulletin board and leave it there for students to see each day, or you can "ditto" copies for each student to have. In either case, you should advise students to become very familiar with the reading assignments so they know what is expected of them.

<u>Extra Activities Center</u> The Extra Activities section of this unit contains suggestions for an extra library of related books and articles in your classroom as well as crossword and word search puzzles. Make an extra activities center in your room where you will keep these materials for students to use. (Bring the books and articles in from the library and keep several copies of the puzzles on hand.) Explain to students that these materials are available for students to use when they finish reading assignments or other class work early.

<u>Nonfiction Assignment Sheet</u> Explain to students that they each are to read at least one non-fiction piece from the in-class library at some time during the unit. Students will fill out a nonfiction assignment sheet after completing the reading to help you evaluate their reading experiences and to help the students think about and evaluate their own reading experiences.

<u>Books</u> Each school has its own rules and regulations regarding student use of school books. Advise students of the procedures that are normal for your school.

<u>Activity #3</u>
Preview the study questions and have students do the vocabulary work for Chapters 1-2 of *The Pigman*. If students do not finish this assignment during this class period, they should complete it prior to the next class meeting.

NONFICTION ASSIGNMENT SHEET
(To be completed after reading the required nonfiction article)

Name _____ Date _____

Title of Nonfiction Read _____

Written By _____ Publication Date _____

I. Factual Summary: Write a short summary of the piece you read.

II. Vocabulary
    1. With which vocabulary words in the piece did you encounter some degree of difficulty?

    2. How did you resolve your lack of understanding with these words?

III. Interpretation: What was the main point the author wanted you to get from reading his work?

IV. Criticism
    1. With which points of the piece did you agree or find easy to accept? Why?

    2. With which points of the piece did you disagree or find difficult to believe? Why?

V. Personal Response: What do you think about this piece? OR How does this piece influence your ideas?

LESSON TWO

<u>Objectives</u>
1. To read chapters 1-2
2. To give students practice reading orally
3. To evaluate students' oral reading
4. To preview the study questions for chapters 3-6
5. To do the prereading vocabulary work for chapters 3-6

<u>Activity</u>

Have students read chapters 1-2 of *The Pigman* out loud in class. You probably know the best way to get readers with your class; pick students at random, ask for volunteers, or use whatever method works best for your group. If you have not yet completed an oral reading evaluation for your students this marking period, this would be a good opportunity to do so. A form is included with this unit for your convenience.

If students do not complete reading chapters 1-2 in class, they should do so prior to your next class meeting.

Also tell students that prior to the next class meeting, they should have previewed the study questions and done the vocabulary worksheets for chapters 3-6.

LESSON THREE

Objectives
    1. To review the main events and ideas from chapters 1-2
    2. To read chapters 3-6
    3. To do the prereading and reading work for chapters 7-9

Activity #1
    Give students a few minutes to formulate answers for the study guide questions for chapters 1-2 and then discuss the answers to the questions in detail. Write the answers on the board or overhead transparency so students can have the correct answers for study purposes. NOTE: It is a good practice in public speaking and leadership skills for individual students to take charge of leading the discussions of the study questions. Perhaps a different student could go to the front of the class and lead the discussion each day that the study questions are discussed during this unit. Of course, the teacher should guide the discussion when appropriate and be sure to fill in any gaps the students leave.

Activity #2
    Have students read chapters 3-6 of *The Pigman* out loud in class. You probably know the best way to get readers with your class; pick students at random, ask for volunteers, or use whatever method works best for your group. Continue the oral reading evaluations.

Activity #3
    Tell students that in your next class period you will be going to the library to work on an assignment. However, prior to the class period after that, they should have completed the prereading and reading work for chapters 7-9. (Give students a specific day by which this assignment must be done.)

ORAL READING EVALUATION - *The Pigman*

Name _____ Class ____ Date _____

SKILL	EXCELLENT	GOOD	AVERAGE	FAIR	POOR
Fluency	5	4	3	2	1
Clarity	5	4	3	2	1
Audibility	5	4	3	2	1
Pronunciation	5	4	3	2	1
_____	5	4	3	2	1
_____	5	4	3	2	1

Total ____ Grade ____

Comments:

LESSON FOUR

Objective:
> To make the project assignment and to give students the time and opportunity to begin working on that assignment

Activity #1
> Distribute the Project Assignment Sheet. Discuss the directions in detail.

Activity #2
> Take your class to the school library so they may begin gathering materials for their projects.

LESSON FIVE

Objectives
> 1. To check to see that students read chapters 7-9 as assigned
> 2. To review the main ideas and events from chapters 3-6 and 7-9
> 3. To preview the study questions for chapters 10-12
> 4. To familiarize students with the vocabulary in chapters 10-12
> 5. To read chapters 10-12

Activity #1
> Quiz - Distribute quizzes and give students about 15 minutes to complete them. (NOTE: The quizzes may either be the short answer study guides or the multiple choice version.) Have students exchange papers. Grade the quizzes as a class. Collect the papers for recording the grades. (If you used the multiple choice version as a quiz, take a few minutes to discuss the answers for the short answer version if your students are using the short answer version for their study guides.)

Activity #2
> Give students the remainder of the class period to preview the study questions, do the related vocabulary work, and read chapters 10-12.

PROJECT ASSIGNMENT SHEET - *The Pigman*

PROMPT

As you already know, Mr. Pignati is called The Pigman because he collects glass, clay and marble pigs. There are many reasons for collecting things: the things collected may have sentimental or monetary value, or perhaps collecting them is just plain fun. Our society even collects things: think of all the museums that hold works of art, manuscripts, antiques, items collected from battlefields, scientific and cultural memorabilia, and so on. Collecting can be an occupation. For example archaeologists dig to find and preserve pieces of mankind's past. Most often though, collecting is a hobby. People collect stamps, cans, coins, postcards--almost anything you can think of!

Collecting is just one of an almost infinite number of hobbies people have. Hobbies fulfill an important role in our lives; they give us personal satisfaction, let us explore things we enjoy--things we may not be able to do for a living but interest us, and they give us something to do in our spare time.

What are your hobbies? What do you like to do in your spare time?

Your assignment is to create a presentation about one of your hobbies for the class. If you do not have any hobbies, think about your parents and others in the community. What are their hobbies? Pick one that most interests you, and do your presentation about that hobby.

REQUIREMENTS

1. Your presentation must last between 4 and 6 minutes.
2. You must read nonfiction information related to the hobby and fill out a Nonfiction Reading Assignment Sheet which will be turned in on the day of your presentation.
3. Your presentation must be in three parts:
    a. approximately 1 minute of explanation in which you tell what the hobby is and how you became interested in it
    b. approximately 3 minutes of showing/demonstrating the hobby
    c. approximately 1 minute of explanation in which you tell why you enjoy this hobby and what you hope to do with it in the future

SUGGESTIONS

1. If your hobby is something that cannot be demonstrated in the classroom (such as skate-boarding, roller-blading, swimming, visiting battlefields, etc.) make a three-minute videotape showing the hobby and show the videotape during the presentation.

2. Since five minutes is a very short time to present something about which you could probably talk for hours, plan your presentation carefully to show the highlights of your hobby. This is also practice in picking out the most important ideas from a whole bunch of information.

3. Bring whatever "props" you need for demonstrating your hobby to class on the day of your presentation. Have everything "ready to go" so you don't waste valuable time looking for things; mark pages in books, lay out things in the order you will need them prior to taking the floor, have your videotape or audio tapes wound to the exact beginning of the demonstration, be dressed in the appropriate attire when you get to class, etc.

LESSON SIX

Objectives
1. To give students the opportunity to practice writing to inform
2. To give students the opportunity to write about a subject in which they are interested
3. To encourage logical thinking
4. To give the teacher the opportunity to evaluate students' writing skills
5. To help prepare students for their presentations
6. To review the main ideas and events from chapters 10-12

Activity #1
Give students a few minutes to formulate answers for the study guide questions for chapters 10-12 and then discuss the answers to the questions in detail. Write the answers on the board or overhead transparency so students can have the correct answers for study purposes.

Activity #2
Pair students in your class. For this assignment, one student can use the other student as the specific audience for his/her composition.

Distribute Writing Assignment #1 and discuss the directions in detail. Allow the remaining class time for students to complete the assignment.

Follow-Up: After you have graded the assignments, have a writing conference with the students. (This unit schedules one in Lesson Ten.) After the writing conference, allow students to revise their papers using your suggestions and corrections. Give them about three days from the date they receive their papers to complete the revision. I suggest grading the revisions on an A-C-E scale (all revisions well-done, some revisions made, few or no revisions made). This will speed your grading time and still give some credit for the students' efforts.

Activity #2
Tell students that prior to the next class period they should have previewed the study questions for, done the vocabulary for, and read chapters 13-15. If they have time after completing the writing assignment, they may begin this reading assignment in class.

WRITING ASSIGNMENT #1 - *The Pigman*

PROMPT

You have been paired with another student in your class. This is not a group assignment; rather, you are to use the other person you are paired with as the audience for your composition. Your partner has just heard about your hobby and is interested in it. He/she has asked you to tell him/her more about your hobby, how to begin having this as a hobby, and what to do. Your assignment is to write a composition in which you explained these things to your classmate.

PREWRITING

What is your hobby? Jot it down on the top of a piece of paper.
Make a few notes describing exactly what your hobby is.
Make a list of things a person would need to get started doing your hobby.
Make a list of things one does after one learns the basics of your hobby. What kinds of things does one who is advanced in this hobby do?
Make a list of reasons why you enjoy this hobby.

DRAFTING

Write an introductory paragraph in which you thank your partner for his/her interest in your hobby and for asking you about it.

Write one paragraph (at least) describing your hobby. Exactly what *is* it? Give details. Refer to your notes for guidance.

Write one paragraph (at least) explaining how one gets started in this hobby, including mentioning any equipment, materials, or memberships that are necessary.

Write one paragraph (at least) explaining what one does after one has begun and has learned the basics of the hobby.

Write a concluding paragraph in which you explain why you enjoy this hobby and wish your partner well if he/she decides to pursue this hobby.

PROMPT

When you finish the rough draft of your paper, ask a student who sits near you to read it. After reading your rough draft, he/she should tell you what he/she liked best about your work, which parts were difficult to understand, and ways in which your work could be improved. Reread your paper considering your critic's comments and make the corrections you think are necessary.

PROOFREADING

Do a final proofreading of your paper double-checking your grammar, spelling, organization, and the clarity of your ideas.

LESSON SEVEN

Objectives
1. To review the main ideas of chapters 13-15
2. To review the vocabulary work done in this unit

Activity #1

Ask students to get out their books and some paper (not their study guides). Tell students to write down ten questions (and answers) which cover the main events and ideas in chapters 13-15. Discuss the students questions and answers orally, making a list of the questions with brief responses on the board. Put a star next to the students' questions and answers that are essentially the same as the study guide questions. (Be sure that all the study guide questions are answered.)

Activity #2

Choose one or more of the vocabulary review activities listed on the next page and spend your class period as directed in the activity. Some of the materials for these review activities are located in the Vocabulary Resource Materials at the end of this unit.

LESSON EIGHT

Objective:
To discuss *The Pigman* on interpretive and critical levels

Activity #1

Choose the questions from the Extra Discussion Questions/Writing Assignments which seem most appropriate for your students. A class discussion of these questions is most effective if students have been given the opportunity to formulate answers to the questions prior to the discussion. To this end, you may either have all the students formulate answers to all the questions, divide your class into groups and assign one or more questions to each group, or you could assign one question to each student in your class. The option you choose will make a difference in the amount of class time needed for this activity.

Activity #3

After students have had ample time to formulate answers to the questions, begin your class discussion of the questions and the ideas presented by the questions. Be sure students take notes during the discussion so they have information to study for the unit test.

VOCABULARY REVIEW ACTIVITIES

1. Divide your class into two teams and have an old-fashioned spelling or definition bee.

2. Give each of your students (or students in groups of two, three or four) a *The Pigman* Vocabulary Word Search Puzzle. The person (group) to find all of the vocabulary words in the puzzle first wins.

3. Give students a *The Pigman* Vocabulary Word Search Puzzle without the word list. The person or group to find the most vocabulary words in the puzzle wins.

4. Use a *The Pigman* Vocabulary Crossword Puzzle. Put the puzzle onto a transparency on the overhead projector (so everyone can see it), and do the puzzle together as a class.

5. Give students a *The Pigman* Vocabulary Matching Worksheet to do.

6. Divide your class into two teams. Use *The Pigman* vocabulary words with their letters jumbled as a word list. Student 1 from Team A faces off against Student 1 from Team B. You write the first jumbled word on the board. The first student (1A or 1B) to unscramble the word wins the chance for his/her team to score points. If 1A wins the jumble, go to student 2A and give him/her a definition. He/she must give you the correct spelling of the vocabulary word which fits that definition. If he/she does, Team A scores a point, and you give student 3A a definition for which you expect a correctly spelled matching vocabulary word. Continue giving Team A definitions until some team member makes an incorrect response. An incorrect response sends the game back to the jumbled-word face off, this time with students 2A and 2B. Instead of repeating giving definitions to the first few students of each team, continue with the student after the one who gave the last incorrect response on the team. For example, if Team B wins the jumbled-word face-off, and student 5B gave the last incorrect answer for Team B, you would start this round of definition questions with student 6B, and so on. The team with the most points wins!

7. Have students write a story in which they correctly use as many vocabulary words as possible. Have students read their compositions orally! Post the most original compositions on your bulletin board.

EXTRA WRITING ASSIGNMENTS/DISCUSSION QUESTIONS - *The Pigman*

Interpretation

1. Explain how Paul Zindel's using both Lorraine and John as the narrators affects our understanding of the events in *The Pigman*.

2. Where is the climax of the story?

3. Explain the importance of the setting in *The Pigman*. Could it have been set in a different time and place and still have had the same effect? Explain your answer.

4. What are the main conflicts in the story and how are they resolved?

Critical

5. Describe Mr. Pignati's relationship with John and Lorraine and contrast it with their relationships with their parents.

6. Are John and Lorraine's actions believably motivated? Explain why or why not.

7. Explain the significance of the fact that both John and Lorraine chose "magic" as being most important in their lives.

8. Characterize Paul Zindel's style of writing. How does it contribute to the value of the novel?

9. Compare and contrast John and Lorraine.

10. Compare and contrast John's parents and Lorraine's mother.

11. Explain how Paul Zindel uses monkeys and baboons to make his points about people.

12. Explain the significance of John and Lorraine's dressing up in Mr. and Mrs. Pignati's clothes.

13. Explain Norton's role in the novel. Why was he included?

14. Discuss the use of nicknames in *The Pigman*, especially The Bore, Bathroom Bomber, Old Lady, Marshmallow Kid, Cricket, and The Pigman.

15. Are the characters in *The Pigman* stereotypes? If so, explain why Paul Zindel used stereotypes. If not, explain how the characters merit individuality.

The Pigman Extra Discussion Questions page 2

<u>Critical/Personal Response</u>

16. *The Pigman* was first published in 1968. Are the characters in this book like real teenagers today? Explain how they are alike and/or how they are different.

17. Much of *The Pigman* tells about John and Lorraine's "free time," time out of school. Compare/contrast their activities with your own free time activities.

18. How would this story and its effect have changed if Mr. Pignati's wife had been living?

19. Do you think the relationship between John and Lorraine is realistic? Explain why or why not.

20. Who is responsible for Mr. Pignati's death?

21. What faults in our society does Paul Zindel point out in *The Pigman?*

22. Consider all the references and inferences made about school in the book. What do you think is Mr. Zindel's opinion of school? What is yours?

23. The book is titled *The Pigman.* Who is the central character of the book? Why?

24. If you had to pick one thing John and Lorraine really shouldn't have done, which one would you pick? What one thing was their biggest mistake?

25. Who was responsible for John and Lorraine's behavior?

26. Suppose this story had been written from Mr. Pignati's point of view. How would the themes have changed?

<u>Personal Response</u>

27. Did you enjoy reading *The Pigman*? Why or why not?

28. Why do some people make crank phone calls?

29. Do you know anyone like Mr. Pignati?

30. Is this story like any other story you have ever read or any movie you may have seen? How are they alike?

LESSON NINE

Objectives
>   1. To review ideas presented in the novel
>   2. To show students specific passages in the novel that are important to theme and/or character development
>   3. To look more closely at Paul Zindel's use of language

Activity

Distribute the Quotations Worksheet. Assign each student one quotation. Tell students that they are to think about their quotations and try to think of some reasons why their quotations would be significant to the theme or character development in the novel.

After giving students a few minutes to think, begin discussing each quotation, using the students' thoughts as a springboard.

QUOTATIONS WORKSHEET - *The Pigman*

1. Lorraine remembers the big words, and I remember the action. (3)

2. . . . if Lorraine felt like saying one of us murdered Mr. Pignati, she should have blamed Norton. He is the one who finally caused all the trouble. (5)

3. "Kenneth never gave us any trouble," she just had to add, neatly folding the polishing rag. (5)

4. You never wanted to visit lonely people before, or is it that you only like lonely people who have ten dollars? (5)

5. You think you're the perfect headshrinker with all those psychology books you read, and you really don't know a thing. (5)

6. I refused to talk to him for five minutes while I drank a chocolate drink I bought with my own money while John cashed the check and got a six-pack of beer and a pack of cigarettes. (6)

7. I can't tell you what she'd do if I ever took anything, but she isn't even ashamed of what she does. (6)

8. I think it'd be a good idea if you stayed home from school and cleaned the house with me tomorrow. (6)

9. I know just how the minds of animals work -- just the kind of games they like to play. (6)

10. The only difference between her fibs and mine are that hers are eerie -- she's got a gift for saying things that make you anxious. (7)

Pigman Quotations Worksheet Page 2

11. It was sort of nice that a baboon had a friend like Mr. Pignati. (7)

12. Maybe you'd better go over to a friend's house to do your homework? (7)

13. I'd wish my mother were more like him. I'd wish she knew how to have a little fun for a change. (8)

14. It's sort of spooky how when you're caught talking to God nowadays everybody thinks you're nuts. They used to call you a Prophet. (8)

15. "I'm not his daughter, " I blurted out. . . . "I'm his niece," I quickly offered. (8)

16. I mean, they lost the whole point of having a ship in a bottle. (8)

17. The three monkeys were hugging each other desperately. . . . Here they were, clinging to each other in the pet shop at Beekman's looking out at everybody with those tiny, wet eyes – as though pleading for love. They looked so lonely and sweet just holding on to each other. (8)

18. One part was saying, "Don't let this nice old man waste his money," and the other half was saying "Enjoy it, enjoy doing something absolutely absurd" . . . . (8)

19. We just had to be honest with you because we like you more than anyone else we know. (10)

20. Maybe there are some lies you should never admit to. (10)

21. They ought to bury people in hospitals and let sick people get well in the cemeteries. (11)

22. His hair was combed for the first time in months, and he actually had on a clean shirt. (12)

Pigman Quotations Worksheet Page 3

23. It's the Pigman who has to forgive me -- not you! (14)

24. I wanted to put my hands to my ears to shut out the jungle that had surrounded us. (14)

25. The lady with a baby in her arms just sneaked out a door. (15)

26. Maybe we were all baboons for that matter -- big blabbing baboons -- smiling away and not really caring what was going on as long as there were enough peanuts bouncing around to think about . . . baffled baboons concentrating on all the wrong things. (15)

27. Maybe I would rather be dead than turn into the kind of grown-up people I knew. What was so hot about living anyway if people think you're a disturbing influence just because you still think about God and Death and the Universe and Love. (15)

28. A whole crowd of people had gathered to crane their necks and watch them roll a dead man onto a stretcher. (15)

29. When you grow up, you're not supposed to go back. Trespassing -- that's what he had done. (15)

30. We had trespasses too -- been where we didn't belong, and we were being punished for it. (15)

31. There was no one else to blame anymore. . . . And there was no place to hide -- no place across any river for a boatman to take us. (15)

32. They build their own cages, we could almost hear the Pigman whisper, as he took his children with him. (15)

LESSON TEN

Objectives
    1. To work with students one on one and evaluate their writing skills
    2. To give students the opportunity to practice writing to persuade

Activity #1
    Distribute Writing Assignment #2. Discuss the directions in detail and give students the remainder of the class period to do the assignment.

Activity #2
    While students are working on Writing Assignment #2, call individual students to your desk or some other private area where you can discuss the students' Writing Assignment #1. A Writing Evaluation Form is provided to help you structure your writing conferences.

WRITING ASSIGNMENT #2 - *The Pigman*

PROMPT

Everyone knows someone who has done something they shouldn't have done. Most of us have been with some friends or acquaintances who have done things they shouldn't have done. Maybe we participated; maybe we didn't. The point is that everyone present and anyone who found out about the situation knew that what was done was wrong to do.

How many people have the courage to stand up and say, "Don't do that!" Most people don't. Most people drift along with the crowd or at best remove themselves from the situation without trying to actually stop others from doing something wrong. Why is that? Maybe out of fear for personal safety, maybe out of fear of not being accepted or not having any friends. Maybe one of a dozen other reasons.

Your assignment is to think of some time when you knew someone was going to do something wrong and write a composition in which you write what you could have said to persuade that person against carrying out his/her plans. Please do not use the people's real names.

PREWRITING

First, you have to think of a time when you knew someone was going to do something wrong . If you honestly can't think of an example, think of some event you heard about after it was done and use that scenario for your composition.

Jot down the details of the situation.

Jot down reasons why the person/people were going to do what they did.

Jot down any thoughts you have about why they shouldn't have done it.

Jot down any thoughts you have about what might have persuaded them not to do it.

DRAFTING

Write a paragraph in which you introduce the details of the situation and explain what was going on. Then, in a letter format, write what you could have said to persuade the person against carrying out his/her plans.

In the first paragraph of your letter, be sure to state what the problem is and that you are against the idea.

In the body of your letter, devote one paragraph for each of the reasons why the person should not carry out his/her plans.

Write a concluding paragraph in which you summarize your points and close your part of the conversation.

PROMPT

When you finish the rough draft of your paper, ask a student who sits near you to read it. After reading your rough draft, he/she should tell you what he/she liked best about your work, which parts were difficult to understand and ways in which your work could be improved. Reread your paper considering your critic's comments, and make the corrections you think are necessary. Do a final proofreading of your paper double-checking your grammar, spelling, organization, and the clarity of your ideas.

WRITING EVALUATION FORM - *The Pigman*

Name _____ Date _____

    Grade _____

Circle One For Each Item:

Grammar: correct   errors noted on paper

Spelling: correct   errors noted on paper

Punctuation: correct   errors noted on paper

Legibility: excellent   good   fair   poor

Strengths:

Weaknesses:

Comments/Suggestions:

LESSON ELEVEN

Objectives
1. To further discuss the ideas presented in the book
2. To give students a chance to work together in small groups to exchange ideas and find information

Activity #1
Divide your class into 10 groups--one group for each of the following ideas:
1. Death/life
2. Lying/truth
3. Role of parents
4. Role of friends
5. Blame/responsibility
6. Character development of John
7. Character development of Lorraine
8. Nicknames
9. Individualism
10. Loneliness

(NOTE: These are some suggestions for topics; feel free to add to or delete from this list.)

Students within the group should prepare to "teach" their topic as it relates to *The Pigman*. They should find relevant passages and come to some reasonable conclusions about their topic as it relates to the book. One student in the group should be appointed secretary/spokesperson to write down and report the group's ideas.

Activity #2
Call on the groups to report the information they were able to compile. Jot the main points down briefly for students to copy into their notes. Use this as a springboard to discuss each of the topics above.

LESSON TWELVE

Objectives
1. To complete the group reports and theme discussions from Lesson Eleven
2. To allow students time to review, compare and correct their notes

Activity #1
Complete the group reports and theme discussions from Lesson Eleven.

Activity #2
Allow any remaining time for students to review, compare, and/or correct their notes.

LESSONS THIRTEEN AND FOURTEEN

Objectives:
1. To conclude the project assignment
2. To give students the chance to show off their hobbies and things they are proud of
3. To show students a wide variety of constructive activities for their free time
4. To give students practice doing public speaking

Activity

Use these class periods for students to give their presentations about their hobbies to conclude the project assignment.

LESSON FIFTEEN

Objectives:
1. To give students the opportunity to express their own personal opinions
2. To get students to take ideas out of the story and apply them to real life
3. To see what students think about responsibilities of the individual to society

Activity

Distribute Writing Assignment #3. Discuss the directions in detail and give students this class period to work on the assignment.

LESSON SIXTEEN

Objectives:
    To review the main ideas and events presented in *The Pigman*.

Activity #1

Choose one of the review games/activities included in this unit and spend your class period as outlined there. Some materials for these activities are located in the Extra Activities section of this unit.

Activity #2

Remind students that the Unit Test will be in the next class meeting. Stress the review of the Study Guides and their class notes as a last-minute, brush-up review for homework.

WRITING ASSIGNMENT #3 - *The Pigman*

PROMPT

During their escapades in this novel, John and Lorraine aren't always model citizens. They lie and cheat and do just about anything they please in the name of "just having fun." Think about this for a minute. What would our lives be like if everyone went around doing just exactly whatever they wanted to do "just having fun"? Would you like to live in a country where people could come in and ruin your favorite things and trash your house while you were out, where people lie and cheat you out of your money on a whim, or where people would just play nasty little tricks on you all the time?

Your assignment is to write a composition in which you answer this question, "What is an individual's responsibility to society?"

PREWRITING

Think about it. What are *your* responsibilities to society? Jot down your ideas.

DRAFTING

Write an introductory paragraph in which you answer the question.

In the body of your composition, write one paragraph for each of the points you want to make, each of the responsibilities a person has to society.

Write a concluding paragraph in which you assess how well most people adhere to their responsibilities today.

PROMPT

When you finish the rough draft of your paper, ask a student who sits near you to read it. After reading your rough draft, he/she should tell you what he/she liked best about your work, which parts were difficult to understand, and ways in which your work could be improved. Reread your paper considering your critic's comments and make the corrections you think are necessary.

PROOFREADING

Do a final proofreading of your paper double-checking your grammar, spelling, organization, and the clarity of your ideas.

REVIEW GAMES/ACTIVITIES - *The Pigman*

1. Ask the class to make up a unit test for *The Pigman*. The test should have 4 sections: matching, true/false, short answer, and essay. Students may use 1/2 period to make the test and then swap papers and use the other 1/2 class period to take a test a classmate has devised. (open book) You may want to use the unit test included in this packet or take questions from the students' unit tests to formulate your own test.

2. Take 1/2 period for students to make up true and false questions (including the answers). Collect the papers and divide the class into two teams. Draw a big tic-tac-toe board on the chalk board. Make one team X and one team O. Ask questions to each side, giving each student one turn. If the question is answered correctly, that students' team's letter (X or O) is placed in the box. If the answer is incorrect, no mark is placed in the box. The object is to get three marks in a row like tic-tac-toe. You may want to keep track of the number of games won for each team.

3. Take 1/2 period for students to make up questions (true/false and short answer). Collect the questions. Divide the class into two teams. You'll alternate asking questions to individual members of teams A & B (like in a spelling bee). The question keeps going from A to B until it is correctly answered, then a new question is asked. A correct answer does not allow the team to get another question. Correct answers are +2 points; incorrect answers are -1 point.

4. Have students pair up and quiz each other from their study guides and class notes.

5. Give students a *The Pigman* crossword puzzle to complete.

6. Divide your class into two teams. Use *The Pigman* crossword words with their letters jumbled as a word list. Student 1 from Team A faces off against Student 1 from Team B. You write the first jumbled word on the board. The first student (1A or 1B) to unscramble the word wins the chance for his/her team to score points. If 1A wins the jumble, go to student 2A and give him/her a clue. He/she must give you the correct word which matches that clue. If he/she does, Team A scores a point, and you give student 3A a clue for which you expect another correct response. Continue giving Team A clues until some team member makes an incorrect response. An incorrect response sends the game back to the jumbled-word face off, this time with students 2A and 2B. Instead of repeating giving clues to the first few students of each team, continue with the student after the one who gave the last incorrect response on the team. For example, if Team B wins the jumbled-word face-off, and student 5B gave the last incorrect answer for Team B, you would start this round of clue questions with student 6B, and so on. The team with the most points wins!

UNIT TESTS

SHORT ANSWER UNIT TEST 1 - *The Pigman*

I. Matching/Identify

___ 1. The Bore   A. John's Mother

___ 2. Bathroom Bomber   B. Norton

___ 3. Old Lady   C. The Librarian

___ 4. Marshmallow Kid   D. John's father

___ 5. Cricket   E. School Friend of John and Lorraine

___ 6. Bobo   F. John

___ 7. The Pigman   G. A baboon

___ 8. Dennis   H. Mr. Pignati

II. Short Answer

1. How did Lorraine and John first encounter Mr. Pignati?

2. Why did John lie to Dennis and Norton about the call to Mr. Pignati?

3. Why did John and Lorraine call Mr. Pignati the Pigman?

4. Why does John say he thinks he is really looking for a ghost?

The Pigman Short Answer Unit Test 1 Page 2

5. Why does John's father say, "Thank God Kenneth isn't a lunatic"?

6. Why does Norton threaten to go to Mr. Pignati's house?

7. How do we know Lorraine's mother is suspicious? Why does Lorraine keep getting away with lies?

8. John and Lorraine tell the police that they are Mr. Pignati's children. Why?

9. Describe the Friday night party at Mr. Pignati's house.

10. Why did Lorraine and John want to take Mr. Pignati to the zoo after the party?

The Pigman Short Answer Unit Test 1 Page 3

III. Composition

What is the point of *The Pigman*? When we read books, we usually come away from our reading experience a little richer, having given more thought to a particular aspect of life. What do you think Paul Zindel intended us to gain from reading his novel?

The Pigman Short Answer Unit Test 1 Page 4

IV. Vocabulary

Listen to the vocabulary word and write them down. Go back later and fill in he correct definition for each word.

1.

2.

3.

4.

5.

6.

7.

8.

9.

10.

SHORT ANSWER UNIT TEST 2 - *The Pigman*

I. Matching

___ 1. The Bore   A. School Friend of John and Lorraine

___ 2. Bathroom Bomber   B. A baboon

___ 3. Old Lady   C. Mr. Pignati

___ 4. Marshmallow Kid   D. John's father

___ 5. Cricket   E. John's Mother

___ 6. Bobo   F. John

___ 7. The Pigman   G. Norton

___ 8. Dennis   H. The Librarian

II. Short Answer

1. Compare and contrast John and Lorraine.

2. How did Lorraine and John first encounter Mr. Pignati?

The Pigman Short Answer Unit Test 2 Page 2

3. Why does John say he thinks he is really looking for a ghost?

4. Why did John and Lorraine confess that they were not charity workers?

5. John and Lorraine tell the police that they are Pignati's children. Why?

6. Mr. Pignati told the kids to take care of what two things until he returned? Did they?

7. What did John want to do that Friday night before Mr. Pignati was due to come home? What actually happened instead?

8. Give two examples of the life/death theme in *The Pigman*.

9. Give two examples of the theme of individualism in *The Pigman*.

10. Give two examples of the theme of loneliness in *The Pigman*.

The Pigman Short Answer Unit Test 2 Page 3

III. Quotations   Explain the significance of each of the following quotations:

1. . . . if Lorraine felt like saying one of us murdered Mr. Pignati, she should have blamed Norton. He is the one who finally caused all the trouble. (5)

2. One part was saying, "Don't let this nice old man waste his money," and the other half was saying "Enjoy it, enjoy doing something absolutely absurd" . . . . (8)

3. We just had to be honest with you because we like you more than anyone else we know. (10)

4. Maybe there are some lies you should never admit to. (10)

5. Maybe we were all baboons for that matter -- big blabbing baboons -- smiling away and not really caring what was going on as long as there were enough peanuts bouncing around to think about . . . baffled baboons concentrating on all the wrong things. (15)

6. When you grow up, you're not supposed to go back. Trespassing -- that's what he had done. (15)

7. There was no one else to blame anymore. . . . And there was no place to hide -- no place across any river for a boatman to take us. (15)

The Pigman Short Answer Unit Test 2 Page 4

IV. Vocabulary

Listen to the vocabulary word and write them down. Go back later and fill in the correct definition for each word.

1.

2.

3.

4.

5.

6.

7.

8.

9.

10.

KEY: SHORT ANSWER UNIT TESTS - *The Pigman*

The short answer questions are taken directly from the study guides.
If you need to look up the answers, you will find them in the study guide section.

Answers to the composition questions will vary depending on your
class discussions and the level of your students.

For the vocabulary section of the test, choose ten of the
words from the vocabulary lists to read orally for your students.

The answers to the matching section of the test are below.

Answers to the matching section of the Advanced Short Answer Unit Test
are the same as for Short Answer Unit Test #2.

<u>Test #1</u>
1. D
2. F
3. A
4. B
5. C
6. G
7. H
8. E

<u>Test #2</u>
1. D
2. F
3. E
4. G
5. H
6. B
7. C
8. A

ADVANCED SHORT ANSWER UNIT TEST - *The Pigman*

I. Matching

___ 1. The Bore   A. School Friend of John and Lorraine

___ 2. Bathroom Bomber   B. A baboon

___ 3. Old Lady   C. Mr. Pignati

___ 4. Marshmallow Kid   D. John's father

___ 5. Cricket   E. John's Mother

___ 6. Bobo   F. John

___ 7. The Pigman   G. Norton

___ 8. Dennis   H. The Librarian

II. Short Answer

1. Describe the Pigman's relationship with John and Lorraine and contrast it with their relationships to their parents.

2. Explain how Paul Zindel's using both John and Lorraine as narrators affects our understanding of the events in *The Pigman*.

The Pigman Advanced Short Answer Unit Test Page 2

3. Explain the importance of the fact that both John and Lorraine both chose "magic" as being important in their lives.

4. Who is responsible for Mr. Pignati's death? Justify your answer.

5. How does John change during the course of the story?

6. What are the main conflicts in the story, and how is each resolved?

7. What are three themes in *The Pigman*? Give a short explanation of each.

8. Relate the puzzle of the wife, husband, lover, boatman and assassin to *The Pigman*.

The Pigman Advanced Short Answer Unit Test Page 3

III. Quotations   Explain the significance of the following quotations from *The Pigman*

1. The three monkeys were hugging each other desperately. . . . Here they were, clinging to each other in the pet shop at Beekman's looking out at everybody with those tiny, wet eyes--as though pleading for love. They looked so lonely and sweet just holding on to each other. (8)

2. We just had to be honest with you because we like you more than anyone else we know. (10)

3. Maybe we were all baboons for that matter--big blabbing baboons--smiling away and not really caring what was going on as long as there were enough peanuts bouncing around to think about . . . baffled baboons concentrating on all the wrong things. (15)

4. Maybe I would rather be dead than turn into the kind of grown-up people I knew. What was so hot about living anyway if people think you're a disturbing influence just because you still think about God and Death and the Universe and Love. (15)

5. A whole crowd of people had gathered to crane their necks and watch them roll a dead man onto a stretcher. (15)

6. We had trespassed too--been where we didn't belong, and we were being punished for it. (15)

7. There was no one else to blame anymore. . . . And there was no place to hide -- no place across any river for a boatman to take us. (15)

8. They build their own cages, we could almost hear the Pigman whisper, as he took his children with him. (15)

The Pigman Advanced Short Answer Unit Test Page 4

III. Composition

Horn Book called *The Pigman* "cruelly truthful about the human condition." Using all of your knowledge about the book, write a composition in which you explain that statement.

The Pigman Advanced Short Answer Unit Test Page 5

IV. Vocabulary

Listen to the vocabulary words and write them down. Go back later and write a composition in which you use all of the words. The composition must in some way relate to our unit about *The Pigman*.

MULTIPLE CHOICE UNIT TEST 1 - *The Pigman*

I. Matching

___ 1. The Bore   A. John's Mother

___ 2. Bathroom Bomber   B. Norton

___ 3. Old Lady   C. The Librarian

___ 4. Marshmallow Kid   D. John's father

___ 5. Cricket   E. School Friend of John and Lorraine

___ 6. Bobo   F. John

___ 7. The Pigman   G. A baboon

___ 8. Dennis   H. Mr. Pignati

II. Multiple Choice

1. Which statement best describes John and Lorraine?
    A. John is depressed and lethargic. Lorraine is destructive and violent.
    B. John is destructive and rebellious. Lorraine is analytic and conforming.
    C. John is friendly and creative. Lorraine is intelligent and shy.
    D. John is a model student. Lorraine hates school.

2. How did Lorraine and John first encounter Mr. Pignati?
    A. They met him on a trip to the zoo.
    B. Lorraine's mother was nursing him and told Lorraine about him.
    C. He gave a talk at their school
    D. Lorraine picked his number from the telephone book for a marathon.

3. What were Lorraine's and John's attitudes towards taking Mr. Pignati's $10.
    A. They both wanted to take the money.
    B. John wanted to take the money, but Lorraine didn't
    C. Neither of them wanted to go through with it.
    D. Lorraine wanted to take the money, but John didn't.

The Pigman Multiple Choice Test 1 Page 2

4. Which does not describe Lorraine's mother?
    A. Steals food and money from clients
    B. Alcoholic
    C. Angry because her husband left her
    D. Doesn't value school

5. Why does John say he thinks he is really looking for a ghost?
    A. He wants to test his courage.
    B. He is showing off his bravery to Lorraine.
    C. He will do anything to prove there is an afterlife.
    D. He thinks he can communicate with it.

6. What do we learn about John's father when he says, "Be yourself! Be individualistic! But for God's sake get your hair cut. You look like an oddball."
    A. He has a strange sense of humor.
    B. He says what he thinks people want to hear.
    C. He hates the thought of John being an actor and will do anything to stop him.
    D. He wants John to be an individual but to stay within conventional standards.

7. What did Mr. Pignati ask them to do while he was in the hospital?
    A. Bring him some chocolate covered ants and frogs legs.
    B. Take care of Bobo and the house.
    C. Call the church and ask the priest to come to see him.
    D. Cut school to visit him, because he was afraid of being alone.

III. Quotations
1. "Lorraine remembers the big words, and I remember the action."
    A. Points out the main differences in Lorraine and John's personalities
    B. Shows that Lorraine is smarter than John
    C. Shows the main differences between girls and boys
    D. B & C

2. "I'm not his daughter," I blurted out. . . ."I'm his niece," I quickly offered.
    A. Shows Lorraine's honesty
    B. Shows how Lorraine got caught in a lie
    C. Shows that Lorraine cares for Mr. Pignati
    D. Shows that Lorraine wishes she could have a real family

The Pigman Multiple Choice Test 1 Page 3

3. "The three monkeys were hugging each other desperately. . . .They looked so lonely and sweet just holding on to each other."
    A. Shows how little people know about monkeys; the monkeys were just keeping warm
    B. Is symbolic of Lorraine, John, and Mr. Pignati's situation
    C. Trivializes the reality that those monkeys were being mistreated
    D. Is symbolic of John's situation with his parents

4. "We just had to be honest with you because we like you more than anyone else we know."
    A. Is an ironic way of showing that lies don't pay
    B. Shows that John and Lorraine think it's okay to lie to people you don't like
    C. Shows John and Lorraine really do like Norton
    D. All of the above

5. Maybe we were all baboons for that matter--big blabbing baboons--smiling away and not really caring what was going on as long as there were enough peanuts bouncing around to think about. . . baffled baboons concentrating on all the wrong things.
    A. Means people are just plain stupid
    B. Means people tend to be shallow-- working for material things rather than having a deeper sense of fulfillment from life
    C. Is a simile metaphor apostrophizing personification
    D. All of the above

6. A whole crowd of people had gathered to crane their necks and watch them roll a dead man onto a stretcher.
    A. Shows people's fascination with death and disaster
    B. Illustrates the theme of death/life in the novel
    C. No one paid attention to a lonely widower who would have liked to have had company walking through the zoo, but everyone wanted to see someone who has just dropped dead
    D. All of the above

The Pigman Multiple Choice Test 1 Page 4

7. There was no one else to blame anymore. . . . And there was no place to hide--no place across any river for a boatman to take us.
    A. John and Lorraine knew that they would be caught for murdering Mr. Pignati. They could not go away; there was no one like Mr. Pignati to help them anymore. Nevertheless, they kept their distance from the scene at the zoo.
    B. They realized that no one was to blame. Mr. Pignati was just an old man who died. They just had to face that fact and face the fact that Mr. Pignati, their friend, was really gone.
    C. John and Lorraine realized that they were to blame for Mr. Pignati's death. They had the old man rollerskating and they were responsible for the party that turned Mr. Pignati's home into shambles, ruining all he had left in this world. And they had to live with that fact for the rest of their lives.
    D. None of the above.

The Pigman Multiple Choice Test 1 Page 5

IV. Composition

    What did John and Lorraine learn during their time with Mr. Pignati and following his death? Explain your answer in detail using details from the story to support your ideas whenever possible.

The Pigman Multiple Choice Test 1 Page 6

IV. Vocabulary

___ 1. DELIBERATELY   A. Give financial assistance to

___ 2. INCONGRUOUS   B. Humiliated; embarrassed

___ 3. SUBSIDIZE   C. A microscopic animal in water, soil & as a parasite in other animals

___ 4. AVOCATION   D. Presence of a clot in a blood vessel

___ 5. AMOEBAE   E. Offset; counterbalance; substitution

___ 6. MUNDANE   F. To become overly concerned with one subject

___ 7. FIXATED   G. Electronic instrument that shows movements of voltage & currents

___ 8. EXAGGERATED   H. Stuck together; jelled; solidified

___ 9. COMPENSATION   I. Ordinary; boring

___ 10. BERSERK   J. Hobby; work; profession

___ 11. GESTURED   K. Mentally or emotionally upset; deranged

___ 12. ARTILLERY   L. Giving off visible light as a result of being heated

___ 13. OSCILLOSCOPE   M. Large caliber weapons

___ 14. CONGEALED   N. Psychological disorder

___ 15. SCHIZOPHRENIC   O. Extreme, irrational distrust of others

___ 16. MORTIFIED   P. Intentionally; on purpose

___ 17. PARANOIA   Q. Enlarged or increased to an abnormal degree

___ 18. THROMBOSIS   R. Incompatible; not belonging together

___ 19. DISMEMBER   S. Motioned with hands

___ 20. INCANDESCENT   T. Divide into pieces

MULTIPLE CHOICE UNIT TEST 2 - *The Pigman*

I. Matching

___ 1. The Bore				A. School Friend of John and Lorraine

___ 2. Bathroom Bomber		B. A baboon

___ 3. Old Lady				C. Mr. Pignati

___ 4. Marshmallow Kid		D. John's father

___ 5. Cricket				E. John's Mother

___ 6. Bobo				F. John

___ 7. The Pigman			G. Norton

___ 8. Dennis				H. The Librarian

II. Multiple Choice
1. Which statement best describes John and Lorraine?
    A. John is depressed and lethargic. Lorraine is destructive and violent.
    B. John is a model student. Lorraine hates school.
    C. John is friendly and creative. Lorraine is intelligent and shy.
    D. John is destructive and rebellious. Lorraine is analytic and conforming.

2. How did Lorraine and John first encounter Mr. Pignati?
    A. Lorraine picked his number from the telephone book for a marathon.
    B. Lorraine's mother was nursing him and told Lorraine about him.
    C. He gave a talk at their school
    D. They met him on a trip to the zoo.

3. What were Lorraine's and John's attitudes towards taking Mr. Pignati's $10?
    A. They both wanted to take the money.
    B. Neither of them wanted to go through with it.
    C. John wanted to take the money, but Lorraine didn't
    D. Lorraine wanted to take the money, but John didn't.

The Pigman Multiple Choice Test 2 Page 2

4. Which does not describe Lorraine's mother?
    A. Alcoholic
    B. Steals food and money from clients
    C. Angry because her husband left her
    D. Doesn't value school

5. Why does John say he thinks he is really looking for a ghost?
    A. He wants to test his courage.
    B. He will do anything to prove there is an afterlife.
    C. He is showing off his bravery to Lorraine.
    D. He thinks he can communicate with it.

6. What do we learn about John's father when he says, "Be yourself! Be individualistic! But for God's sake get your hair cut. You look like an oddball."
    A. He wants John to be an individual but to stay within conventional standards.
    B. He says what he thinks people want to hear.
    C. He hates the thought of John being an actor and will do anything to stop him.
    D. He has a strange sense of humor.

7. What did Mr. Pignati ask them to do while he was in the hospital?
    A. Bring him some chocolate covered ants and frogs legs.
    B. Call the church and ask the priest to come to see him.
    C. Take care of Bobo and the house.
    D. Cut school to visit him, because he was afraid of being alone.

III. Quotations
1. "Lorraine remembers the big words, and I remember the action."
    A. Shows that Lorraine is smarter than John
    B. Points out the main differences in Lorraine and John's personalities
    C. Shows the main differences between girls and boys
    D. B & C

2. "I'm not his daughter," I blurted out. . . ."I'm his niece," I quickly offered."
    A. Shows that Lorraine cares for Mr. Pignati
    B. Shows how Lorraine got caught in a lie
    C. Shows Lorraine's honesty
    D. Shows that Lorraine wishes she could have a real family

The Pigman Multiple Choice Test 2 Page 3

3. "The three monkeys were hugging each other desperately. . . .They looked so lonely and sweet just holding on to each other."
    - A. Shows how little people know about monkeys; the monkeys were just keeping warm
    - B. Is symbolic of John's situation with his parents
    - C. Trivializes the reality that those monkeys were being mistreated
    - D. Is symbolic of Lorraine, John and Mr. Pignati's situation

4. "We just had to be honest with you because we like you more than anyone else we know."
    - A. Is an ironic way of showing that lies don't pay
    - B. Shows John and Lorraine really do like Norton
    - C. Shows that John and Lorraine think it's okay to lie to people you don't like
    - D. All of the above

5. Maybe we were all baboons for that matter--big blabbing baboons--smiling away and not really caring what was going on as long as there were enough peanuts bouncing around to think about . . . baffled baboons concentrating on all the wrong things.
    - A. Means people tend to be shallow-- working for material things rather than having a deeper sense of fulfillment from life
    - B. Means people are just plain stupid
    - C. Is a simile metaphor apostrophizing personification
    - D. All of the above

6. A whole crowd of people had gathered to crane their necks and watch them roll a dead man onto a stretcher.
    - A. Shows people's fascination with death and disaster
    - B. Illustrates the theme of death/life in the novel
    - C. No one paid attention to a lonely widower who would have liked to have had company walking through the zoo, but everyone wanted to see someone who has just dropped dead
    - D. All of the above

The Pigman Multiple Choice Test 2 Page 4

7. There was no one else to blame anymore. . . . And there was no place to hide--no place across any river for a boatman to take us.
    A. John and Lorraine knew that they would be caught for murdering Mr. Pignati. They could not go away; there was no one like Mr. Pignati to help them anymore. Nevertheless, they kept their distance from the scene at the zoo.
    B. John and Lorraine realized that they were to blame for Mr. Pignati's death. They had the old man rollerskating and they were responsible for the party that turned Mr. Pignati's home into shambles, ruining all he had left in this world. And they had to live with that fact for the rest of their lives.
    C. They realized that no one was to blame. Mr. Pignati was just an old man who died. They just had to face that fact, and face the fact that Mr. Pignati, their friend, was really gone.
    D. None of the above.

The Pigman Multiple Choice Test 2 Page 5

III. Composition

Are John and Lorraine "good guys" or "bad guys"? Justify your answers with specific events and examples from the text.

The Pigman Multiple Choice Test 2 Page 6

IV. Vocabulary

___ 1. RELAPSES   A. Not able to adjust to the demands of personal relationships

___ 2. CONGEALED   B. Mentally or emotionally upset; deranged

___ 3. DELIBERATELY   C. Divide into pieces

___ 4. AMOEBAE   D. Police organization using terroristic methods

___ 5. MORTIFIED   E. Offset; counterbalance; substitution

___ 6. GESTAPO   F. Presence of a clot in a blood vessel

___ 7. MALADJUSTED   G. Give financial assistance to

___ 8. INCANDESCENT   H. Falling back to a former condition

___ 9. DISMEMBER   I. Stuck together; jelled; solidified

___ 10. RITUAL   J. Intentionally; on purpose

___ 11. ANALYZE   K. Humiliated; embarrassed

___ 12. BERSERK   L. Lies; statements straying from the truth

___ 13. GESTURED   M. Giving off visible light as a result of being heated

___ 14. COMPENSATION   N. Large caliber weapons

___ 15. PREDICAMENT   O. Troublesome situation

___ 16. ARTILLERY   P. Ceremony; routine

___ 17. ANTAGONISTIC   Q. A microscopic animal in water, soil & as a parasite in other animals

___ 18. THROMBOSIS   R. Saying or doing things to intentionally annoy or displease someone

___ 19. SUBSIDIZE   S. Motioned with hands

___ 20. PREVARICATIONS   T. Examine methodically

ANSWER SHEET - *The Pigman*
Multiple Choice Unit Tests

I. Matching	II. Multiple Choice	III. Quotes	IV. Vocabulary
1. ___	1. ___	1. ___	1. ___
2. ___	2. ___	2. ___	2. ___
3. ___	3. ___	3. ___	3. ___
4. ___	4. ___	4. ___	4. ___
5. ___	5. ___	5. ___	5. ___
6. ___	6. ___	6. ___	6. ___
7. ___	7. ___	7. ___	7. ___
8. ___			8. ___
			9. ___
			10. ___
			11. ___
			12. ___
			13. ___
			14. ___
			15. ___
			16. ___
			17. ___
			18. ___
			19. ___
			20. ___

ANSWER KEY MULTIPLE CHOICE UNIT TESTS – *The Pigman*

Answers to Unit Test 1 are in the left column. Answers to Unit Test 2 are in the right column.

I. Matching	II. Multiple Choice	III. Quotes	IV. Vocabulary
1. D D	1. B D	1. A B	1. P H
2. F F	2. D A	2. C A	2. R I
3. A E	3. B C	3. B D	3. A J
4. B G	4. B A	4. B C	4. J Q
5. C H	5. C B	5. B A	5. C K
6. G B	6. D A	6. D D	6. I D
7. H C	7. B C	7. C B	7. F A
8. E A			8. Q M
			9. E C
			10. K P
			11. S T
			12. M B
			13. G S
			14. H E
			15. N O
			16. B N
			17. O R
			18. D F
			19. T G
			20. L L

UNIT RESOURCE MATERIALS

BULLETIN BOARD IDEAS - *The Pigman*

1. Save one corner of the board for the best of students' *The Pigman* writing assignments.

2. Take one of the word search puzzles from the extra activities packet and with a marker copy it over in a large size on the bulletin board. Write the clue words to find to one side. Invite students prior to and after class to find the words and circle them on the bulletin board.

3. Write several of the most significant quotations from the book onto the board on brightly colored paper.

4. Make a bulletin board listing the vocabulary words for this unit. As you complete sections of the novel and discuss the vocabulary for each section, write the definitions on the bulletin board. (If your board is one students face frequently, it will help them learn the words.)

5. Draw an enlarged version of Mr. Pignati's game on the board (wife, husband, lover, assassin, boatman) with corresponding passages from the book written next to it.

6. Do a bulletin board about nicknames. Include a picture of the famous person with both the real and nicknames written next to it and a little statement telling for what the person is/was famous.

7. Do a bulletin board about hobbies as directed in Lesson One.

8. Make a bulletin board about Paul Zindel. Post biographical information about him in the center of the board and make cut-out "books" with the titles of his other works written on the fronts to post around the biography.

9. Title the board THE PIGMAN. Invite students to write their comments about the characters and events in the story on the bulletin board for a graffiti-style board throughout the duration of this unit.

10. Title the board THE PIGMAN. Invite students to find, bring in and post as many pictures of pigs as they can find. (Students will, in effect, make their own pig collection!)

EXTRA ACTIVITIES - *The Pigman*

One of the difficulties in teaching a novel is that all students don't read at the same speed. One student who likes to read may take the book home and finish it in a day or two. Sometimes a few students finish the in-class assignments early. The problem, then, is finding suitable extra activities for students.

The best thing I've found is to keep a little library in the classroom. For this unit on *The Pigman,* you might check out from the school library other related books and articles about student/parent relationships, psychology, marriage, death, zoos and animals, pigs, hobbies, etc.

Other things you may keep on hand are puzzles. We have made some relating directly to *The Pigman* for you. Feel free to duplicate them for your class.

Some students may like to draw. You might devise a contest or allow some extra-credit grade for students who draw characters or scenes from *The Pigman*. Note, too, that if the students do not want to keep their drawings you may pick up some extra bulletin board materials this way. If you have a contest and you supply the prize (a CD or something like that perhaps), you could, possibly, make the drawing itself a non-refundable entry fee.

The pages which follow contain games, puzzles, and worksheets. The keys, when appropriate, immediately follow the puzzle or worksheet. There are two main groups of activities: one group for the unit; that is, generally relating to the *The Pigman* text, and another group of activities related strictly to the *The Pigman* vocabulary.

Directions for these games, puzzles and worksheets are self-explanatory. The object here is to provide you with extra materials you may use in any way you choose.

MORE ACTIVITIES - *The Pigman*

1. Pick a chapter or scene with a great deal of dialogue and have the students act it out on a stage. (Perhaps you could assign various scenes to different groups of students so more than one scene could be acted and more students could participate.)

2. Have students keep a diary during this unit. The point of the assignment is to have them copy the first person narrative style as well as to keep in touch with their own thoughts.

4. Have students design a book cover (front and back and inside flaps) for *The Pigman*.

5. Have students design a bulletin board (ready to be put up; not just sketched) for *The Pigman*.

6. Ask each student to bring in a "delicacy" for students to taste.

7. Have students choose one chapter of the play (with sufficient dialogue) to rewrite as a play. In conjunction with this assignment, have students write a composition explaining the difficulties they encountered in changing from one written form to another.

8. Hold a trial of your own in which John and Lorraine go on trial for the murder of Mr. Pignati.

9. Have students in your class organize a "Hobby Fair" for your entire school. Students would have to plan and host the event. One way to do this is to let any student sign up for a little booth or table on which he/she can show off his/her hobby. You could also invite local residents to participate. Perhaps get some local businesses to donate prizes, and make award ribbons for several different categories of hobbies. Depending on the regulations in your area, perhaps some of the participants who make things for their hobbies could sell some of their goods. You can make this as elaborate or as simple as you and your class wish.

10. Make a hotline bulletin board with numbers students can call for advice in case their communications lines are down with their parents and they don't have anyone like Mr. Pignati to turn to.

11. Make a bulletin board about people and animals--the role pets play in our lives as our friends, companions, and helpers.

WORD SEARCH - *The Pigman*

All words in this list are associated with *The Pigman*. The words are placed backwards, forward, diagonally, up and down. The included words are listed below the word searches.

```
C X M G N Y N D S C Q B Z K C A L J H Q X A B Z
X L Q I P G D N P F P X G P L Q N N C F L M L G
V K T N B P E E H V G B C L L R O G J B U D Y B
M A R S H M A L L O W H O W A R D D E A N N A X
L H T P O P O L K I E R S M T T E R B L O R D W
K R O T L M A T L C C G P O B N T V G T O K N G
B O B O A W K F K A L A N I N E P E O N T A E V
Z Z B W S C K I L O B V C I G A R H H L I F S L
T P Y I O C K I N Z Q D S I T S M J J C I S M E
W C J C N W C E L G L S D A E A L G I W N R N R
K H A W S E L S E N A N V O H S K R I S C O D X
F E W M Z Y R R Y S A W M C M R T S T P H N C P
P C N M L J O D S M P X C P F C A U F P A C M G
S L G N G B B A T B H Y Q P E F N V E B K K C J
Y J T V E Y D A L D L O Z L S A Q L S J G Q G C
T L B X V T O T Z D N J E M E X E U S F G S V Y
D R J Y D B H F X R V T F P P T H C R I C K E T
```

AHRA	CHECK	KING	PEANUTS
ALBERT	CONCHETTA	KOBIN	PIGMAN
ALICE	CRICKET	LATIN	PIGS
ANGELO	DEANNA	LONELY	ROLL
ASSASSIN	DELICACIES	LOVER	SKATING
ATTACK	DENNIS	MARSHMALLOW	TELEPHONE
BARON	ELECTRICIAN	NORTON	TOMB
BOATMAN	FUND	ODDBALL	TONY
BOBO	HOWARD	OLDLADY	WALL
BOMBER	HUSBAND	OMENS	WIFE
BORE	KENNETH	PEACOCK	ZOO

CROSSWORD - *The Pigman*

CROSSWORD CLUES - *The Pigman*

ACROSS
1. Money
4. Dear ___
6. Magic
8. School friend of John & Lorraine
10. Mr. Pignati gave the L&J fund one for $10
12. Mother, for short
13. Aunt whose ghost gets blamed
14. ... get your hair cut. You look like an ___.
17. Club Lorraine used as an excuse for not being home
18. Olfactory organ
19. Supercolossal fruit ___
20. A baboon
21. Plural of 'to be'
22. Masterson's ___
23. Past tense of 'get'
24. Opposite of 'less'
27. Sex
28. Urban area
29. The ___; John's father
30. Street where Kenneth works
33. Mr. Pignati
34. L&J got to ---- delicacies
36. L&J didn't have time to --- Mr. P's house
37. John's mother
39. Dennis's last name
42. Complete; end
43. Mr. Pignati's former occupation
44. Dark time
45. Has a habit of shoplifting
46. Noise
47. Love

DOWN
1. Mr. Pignati's first name
2. Omen; signal
3. Bobo's home
4. Mr. Pignati had a heart
5. Mrs. Pignati. She's not in California.
6. ___ Park Zoo ___
7. She fixed the attendance cards for L & J
9. Roller rink activity at Mr Pignati's house
11. John's older brother
12. ___ Kid; Norton
13. The prince in a can
15. What Mr. Pignati buys J & L to eat
16. The librarian
17. These people need visitors
20. Bathroom
25. Lorraine was attacked by a low IQ ___
26. Avenue; Mr. Pignati's street ___
30. Fun
31. ___ marathon
32. ___'s market; sells beer to anyone
33. Food for Bobo
35. What Mr. P may have done to Bobo's head
37. Peanut lady, peacock, & nocturnal room were ___ of a bad day
38. Clever; funny
39. 'Old maid' English teacher
40. Large
41. What Mr. Pignati collects
42. The L & J ___

CROSSWORD ANSWER KEY - *The Pigman*

MATCHING QUIZ/WORKSHEET 1 - *The Pigman*

___ 1. PIGMAN   A. Roller rink activity at Mr Pignati's house

___ 2. KOBIN   B. Food for Bobo

___ 3. AHRA   C. Mr. Pignati

___ 4. SKATING   D. Avenue; Mr. Pignati's street

___ 5. ATTACK   E. Mr. Pignati gave the L&J fund one for $10

___ 6. PEACOCK   F. Mr. Pignati had a heart ___

___ 7. KENNETH   G. Peanut lady, peacock, & nocturnal room were ___ of a bad day

___ 8. DENNIS   H. Bobo's home

___ 9. PEANUTS   I. Supercolossal fruit ____

___ 10. PIGS   J. ___'s market; sells beer to anyone

___ 11. NORTON   K. School friend of John & Lorraine

___ 12. DELICACIES   L. What Mr. Pignati buys J & L to eat

___ 13. ZOO   M. John's older brother

___ 14. TONY   N. Has a habit of shoplifting

___ 15. LOVER   O. ... get your hair cut. You look like an ___.

___ 16. OMENS   P. Aunt whose ghost gets blamed

___ 17. CHECK   Q. What Mr. Pignati collects

___ 18. HOWARD   R. Lorraine was attacked by a low IQ ___

___ 19. ODDBALL   S. Sex

___ 20. ROLL   T. Dennis' last name

MATCHING QUIZ/WORKSHEET 2 - *The Pigman*

___ 1. WALL   A. Supercolossal fruit ____

___ 2. ZOO   B. ____ Kid; Norton

___ 3. NORTON   C. Mr. Pignati's former occupation

___ 4. PIGMAN   D. What Mr. Pignati collects

___ 5. PEANUTS   E. The ___; John's father

___ 6. LONELY   F. What Mr. Pignati buys J & L to eat

___ 7. ALBERT   G. 'Old maid' English teacher

___ 8. DENNIS   H. Street where Kenneth works

___ 9. TONY   I. Mrs. Pignati. She's not in California.

___ 10. LOVER   J. ___'s market; sells beer to anyone

___ 11. ROLL   K. Sex

___ 12. BORE   L. The librarian

___ 13. HUSBAND   M. The prince in a can

___ 14. ELECTRICIAN   N. These people need visitors

___ 15. KING   O. Food for Bobo

___ 16. CRICKET   P. Love

___ 17. MARSHMALLOW   Q. Has a habit of shoplifting

___ 18. PIGS   R. Mr. Pignati

___ 19. CONCHETTA   S. School friend of John & Lorraine

___ 20. DELICACIES   T. Bobo's home

KEY: MATCHING QUIZ/WORKSHEETS - *The Pigman*

Worksheet 1	Worksheet 2
1. C	1. H
2. T	2. T
3. P	3. Q
4. A	4. R
5. F	5. O
6. R	6. N
7. M	7. M
8. K	8. S
9. B	9. B
10. Q	10. K
11. N	11. A
12. L	12. E
13. H	13. P
14. J	14. C
15. S	15. G
16. F	16. L
17. E	17. B
18. D	18. D
19. O	19. I
20. I	20. F

JUGGLE LETTER REVIEW GAME CLUE SHEET - *The Pigman*

SCRAMBLED	WORD	CLUE
OKINB	KOBIN	Dennis' last name
OBER	BORE	The _____; John's father
SNIDEN	DENNIS	School friend of John & Lorraine
LLOR	ROLL	Supercolossal fruit _____
BMOT	TOMB	Masterson's _____
INGK	KING	'Old maid' English teacher
RVEOL	LOVER	Sex
IERTCCK	CRICKET	The librarian
ABMONTA	BOATMAN	Magic
SGIP	PIGS	What Mr. Pignati collects
ECOPAKC	PEACOCK	Lorraine was attacked by a low ID _____
NOLAEG	ANGELO	Mr. Pignati's first name
PNEHLOEET	TELEPHONE	_____ marathon
HRAA	AHRA	Aunt whose ghost gets blamed
CIEAL	ALICE	Dear _____
OBOB	BOBO	A baboon
HKNTNEE	KENNETH	John's older brother
NSTPEAU	PEANUTS	Food for Bobo
KEHCC	CHECK	Mr. Pignati gave the L&J fund one for $10
LCESEIIADC	DELICACIES	What Mr. Pignati buys J&L to eat
RNOONT	NORTON	Has a habit of shoplifting
OZO	ZOO	Bobo's home
AETNCOTCH	CONCHETTA	Mrs. Pignati. She's not in California
SANSSIAS	ASSASSIN	Money
LABDDOL	ODDBALL	....get your hair cut. You look like an _____.
NFDU	FUND	The L & J _____
AMIGNP	PIGMAN	Mr. Pignati
ITANL	LATIN	Club Lorraine used as an excuse for not being home
WDRHAO	HOWARD	Avenue; Mr. Pignati's street
RBONA	BARON	_____ Park Zoo
ATGKNSI	SKATING	Roller rink activity at Mr. Pignati's house
KATCAT	ATTACK	Mr. Piganti had a heart _____
ICCAITENRLE	ELECTRICIAN	Mr. Pignati's former occupation
DLAYLOD	OLDLADY	John's mother
LLWA	WALL	Street where Kenneth works
NADNAE	DEANNA	She fixed the attendance cards for L&J

VOCABULARY RESOURCE MATERIALS

VOCABULARY WORD SEARCH - *The Pigman*

All words in this list are associated with *The Pigman* with an emphasis on the vocabulary words chosen for study in the text. The words are placed backwards, forward, diagonally, up and down. The included words are listed below.

```
E X A G G E R A T E D B T F M O R T I F I E D B
W Q W C Q H P M T G J Y D T I P H V O G S N P Q
X D H M G R L Y D N Q M E B H X I P J P K E Y W
S C H I Z O P H R E N I C P A R A N O I A Q Q Y
Q C G E V V S R S C T T N P O T O T G B H J T R
V Y O M M X G U O P X S V C S C B M E R T B I D
C O Z N X O O E B F R D U E O Z S O B D A T B J
A N L G G M G R S S I E G J M N M O P O U T F C
C R O U T E Z L E T I C D N D A G U L A S M E T
H J T I P V A S O B U D I I I A N R L L D I G V
Z W T I T T P L S B M R I E C T L A U L I P S R
G Y F F L A U V E H I E E Z N A S A L O E C G P
W F B K L L C O T D Q N M D E C M U M Y U D S T
X Z Z E J J E O U Z F P Z S Y Z Y E J G Z S V O
B E R S E R K R V S E T A M I T N I N D C E P J
C B X V H L T T Y A Z B L G W D N X G T A Q G P
M U N D A N E C O M P E N S A T I O N F H H C N
```

ADJUSTING	DISMEMBER	INTIMATE	PROFICIENCY
AMOEBAE	EXAGGERATED	MALADJUSTED	RELAPSES
ANALYZE	FIXATED	MORTIFIED	RITUAL
ARTILLERY	GESTAPO	MULLED	SCHIZOPHRENIC
AVOCATION	GESTURED	MUNDANE	SUBSIDIZE
BERSERK	HEMOGLOBIN	OSCILLOSCOPE	THROMBOSIS
COMPENSATION	INCONGRUOUS	PARANOIA	TITMOUSE
CONGEALED	INGRATE	PREDICAMENT	VOLUPTUOUS

VOCABULARY CROSSWORD - *The Pigman*

VOCABULARY CROSSWORD CLUES - *The Pigman*

ACROSS
2. Thought about; pondered
5. Dear ___
7. Police organization using terroristic methods
10. Large caliber weapons
11. Hobby; work; profession
13. What Mr. Pignati collects
14. 'Old maid' English teacher
15. Examine methodically
18. Ceremony; routine
20. Sex
21. Mr. Pignati's first name
23. Nickname for father
26. Fun
27. Fixing to a more compatible position
28. John & Lorraine were ----; intelligent
30. Falling back to a former condition
32. To become overly concerned with one subject
34. The ___; John's father
36. Offset; counterbalance; substitution
39. Motioned with hands
40. Masterson's ___
41. The prince in a can

DOWN
1. Mr. Pignati gave the L&J fund one for $10
2. Humiliated; embarrassed
3. When a boy and girl go out together ___ courting
4. Supercolossal fruit _
6. Stuck together; jelled; solidified
8. Enlarged or increased to an abnormal degree
9. Mentally or emotionally upset; deranged
10. Saying or doing things to intentionally annoy or displease someone
12. Electronic instrument that shows movements of voltage & currents
16. A microscopic animal in water, soil & as a parasite in other animals
17. Ordinary; boring
19. Intentionally; on purpose
22. Close; personal
24. Divide into pieces ___
25. Give financial assistance to
29. Bathroom
31. ___ Park Zoo
33. A baboon
35. Peanut lady, peacock, & nocturnal room were ___ of a bad day ___
37. Aunt whose ghost gets blamed
38. The L & J

VOCABULARY CROSSWORD ANSWER KEY - *The Pigman*

C								M	U	L	L	E	D		R				A	L	I	C	E
H		G	E	S	T	A	P	O					A		O		B					O	
E			X					R			A	R	T	I	L	L	E	R	Y			N	
C			A	V	O	C	A	T	I	O	N		E		L		R			P	I	G	S
K	I	N	G		S			I			T						S					E	
			G		C			F			A	N	A	L	Y	Z	E			M		A	
			E		I			I			G		M				R	I	T	U	A	L	
	D		R		L	O	V	E	R		O		O				K			N		E	
	E		A		L			D		A	N	G	E	L	O			I		D	A	D	
	L		T		O		D				I		B			S		N		A			
W	I	F	E		S		I				S		A	D	J	U	S	T	I	N	G		
	B		D		C		S	M	A	R	T		E			B		I		E			B
	E				O		M				I					S		M					O
	R	E	L	A	P	S	E	S			C		B		F	I	X	A	T	E	D		M
	A				E		M						A			D		T					B
	T			B			B						R			I		E		B	O	R	E
	E		C	O	M	P	E	N	S	A	T	I	O	N		Z			F		M		R
	L			B			R			H			N		G	E	S	T	U	R	E	D	
	Y		T	O	M	B				R									N		N		
										A	L	B	E	R	T				D		S		

VOCABULARY WORKSHEET 1 - *The Pigman*

___ 1. Hobby; work; profession
    a. Maladjusted   b. Avocation   c. Berserk   d. Mundane

___ 2. Iron-containing respiratory pigment in red blood cells
    a. Amoebae   b. Thrombosis   c. Hemoglobin   d. Exaggerated

___ 3. A microscopic animal in water, soil & as a parasite in other animals
    a. Compensation   b. Incongruous   c. Amoebae   d. Voluptuous

___ 4. Stuck together; jelled; solidified
    a. Congealed   b. Mulled   c. Incongruous   d. Exaggerated

___ 5. Troublesome situation
    a. Predicament   b. Adjusting   c. Exaggerated   d. Mortified

___ 6. Falling back to a former condition
    a. Mulled   b. Mortified   c. Relapses   d. Paranoia

___ 7. Police organization using terroristic methods
    a. Oscilloscope   b. Gestapo   c. Predicament   d. Mulled

___ 8. Psychological disorder
    a. Fixated   b. Proficiency   c. Schizophrenic   d. Incongruous

___ 9. Give financial assistance to
    a. Hemoglobin   b. Ritual   c. Subsidize   d. Dismember

___ 10. Motioned with hands
    a. Voluptuous   b. Gestured   c. Thrombosis   d. Avocation

___ 11. Divide into pieces
    a. Dismember   b. Mulled   c. Adjusting   d. Ritual

___ 12. Intentionally; on purpose
    a. Deliberately   b. Gestured   c. Avocation   d. Amoebae

___ 13. Not able to adjust to the demands of personal relationships
    a. Maladjusted   b. Relapses   c. Ritual   d. Voluptuous

___ 14. Giving off visible light as a result of being heated
    a. Amoebae   b. Proficiency   c. Incandescent   d. Prevarications

___ 15. To become overly concerned with one subject
    a. Artillery   b. Fixated   c. Avocation   d. Deliberately

___ 16. Giving ample, unrestrained pleasure to the senses
    a. Voluptuous   b. Thrombosis   c. Amoebae   d. Ritual

___ 17. Mentally or emotionally upset; deranged
    a. Schizophrenic   b. Subsidize   c. Berserk   d. Paranoia

___ 18. Close; personal
    a. Prevarications   b. Intimate   c. Hemoglobin   d. Gestured

___ 19. Saying or doing things to intentionally annoy or displease someone
    a. Antagonistic   b. Paranoia   c. Intimate   d. Voluptuous

___ 20. Competency; ability to do something well
    a. Hemoglobin   b. Fixated   c. Proficiency   d. Incongruous

VOCABULARY WORKSHEET 2 - *The Pigman*

___ 1. DELIBERATELY A. Give financial assistance to

___ 2. INCONGRUOUS B. Humiliated; embarrassed

___ 3. SUBSIDIZE C. A microscopic animal in water, soil & as a parasite in other animals

___ 4. AVOCATION D. Presence of a clot in a blood vessel

___ 5. AMOEBAE E. Offset; counterbalance; substitution

___ 6. MUNDANE F. To become overly concerned with one subject

___ 7. FIXATED G. Electronic instrument that shows movements of voltage & currents

___ 8. EXAGGERATED H. Stuck together; jelled; solidified

___ 9. COMPENSATION I. Ordinary; boring

___ 10. BERSERK J. Hobby; work; profession

___ 11. GESTURED K. Mentally or emotionally upset; deranged

___ 12. ARTILLERY L. Giving off visible light as a result of being heated

___ 13. OSCILLOSCOPE M. Large caliber weapons

___ 14. CONGEALED N. Psychological disorder

___ 15. SCHIZOPHRENIC O. Extreme, irrational distrust of others

___ 16. MORTIFIED P. Intentionally; on purpose

___ 17. PARANOIA Q. Enlarged or increased to an abnormal degree

___ 18. THROMBOSIS R. Incompatible; not belonging together

___ 19. DISMEMBER S. Motioned with hands

___ 20. INCANDESCENT T. Divide into pieces

KEY: VOCABULARY WORKSHEETS - *The Pigman*

Worksheet 1	Worksheet 2
1. B	1. P
2. C	2. R
3. C	3. A
4. A	4. J
5. A	5. C
6. C	6. I
7. B	7. F
8. C	8. Q
9. C	9. E
10. B	10. K
11. A	11. S
12. A	12. M
13. A	13. G
14. C	14. H
15. B	15. N
16. A	16. B
17. D	17. O
18. B	18. D
19. A	19. T
20. C	20. L

VOCABULARY JUGGLE LETTER REVIEW GAME CLUES - *The Pigman*

SCRAMBLED	WORD	CLUE
DIFROIMTE	MORTIFIED	Humiliated; embarrassed
OEABAEM	AMOEBAE	A microscopic animal in water, soil and as a parasite in other animals
TXADEFI	FIXATED	To become overly concerned with one subject
MRBISOSTHO	THROMBOSIS	Presence of a clot in a blood vessel
TARNIEG	INGRATE	An ungrateful person
PIHSEHIRZOCCN	SCHIZOPHRENIC	Psychological disorder
MTNIAETI	INTIMATE	Close; personal
LLEMDU	MULLED	Thought about; pondered
ESREAPSL	RELAPSES	Falling back to a former condition
RITICAPRNAOSVE	PREVARICATIONS	Lies; statements straying from the truth
EELCADNGO	CONGEALED	Stuck together; jelled; solidified
GTISNAATCOIN	ANTAGONISTIC	Saying or doing things to intentionally annoy or displease someone
ISBMREEMD	DISMEMBER	Divide into pieces
CITECNNNESAD	INCANDESCENT	Giving off visible light as a result of being heated
ROAPIANA	PARANOIA	Extreme, irrational distrust of others
EESRBKR	BERSERK	Mentally or emotionally upset; deranged
AEUMDNN	MUNDANE	Ordinary; boring
IRBTYEEELLAD	DELIBERATELY	Intentionally; on purpose
ULIRTA	RITUAL	Ceremony; routine
NONRICOGUSU	INCONGRUOUS	Incompatible; not belonging together
COOVNIATA	AVOCATION	Hobby; work; profession
IMOUESTT	TITMOUSE	Small insect-eating bird
EMONOBILGH	HEMOGLOBIN	Iron-containing respiratory pigment in red blood cells
DIOMFEITR	MORTIFIED	Humiliated; embarrassed
RTLLIEYAR	ARTILLERY	Large caliber weapons
NSGATIDUJ	ADJUSTING	Fixing to a more compatible position
GAEDEGEXRTA	EXAGGERATED	Enlarged or increased to an abnormal degree
CAPTENDERMI	PREDICAMENT	Troublesome situation
POLSOCCILOES	OSCILLOSCOPE	Electronic instrument that shows movements of voltage and currents
UUOTOSPUVL	VOLUPTUOUS	Giving ample, unrestrained pleasure to the senses
SDMJALETUAD	MALADJUSTED	Not able to adjust to the demands of personal relationships